Business Law

Principles and Practices

SECOND EDITION

STUDY GUIDE

Arnold J. Goldman
William D. Sigismond

Houghton Mifflin Company BOSTON
Dallas Geneva, Ill. Lawrenceville, N.J. Palo Alto

Printed in U.S.A.

ISBN: 0-395-44971-5

EFGHIJ-SM-9643210

Contents

UNIT 1 LAW IN ACTION

Chapter 1 Understanding the Law

NAME________________________________ DATE__________

SCORE__________

Study Guide and Review

PART 1: Indicate whether each statement below is true or false by circling either "true" or "false" in the Answers column.

	ANSWERS		SCORE
1. Law is a set of rules for controlling both individual and group conduct.	true	false	1.______
2. The Uniform Commercial Code (UCC) makes the laws of commercial transactions uniform from one state to another.	true	false	2.______
3. Precedents are prior court rulings used as a basis for deciding later cases.	true	false	3.______
4. *The State of California v. Martin* is an example of a civil lawsuit case title.	true	false	4.______
5. The system granting relief for a wrongdoing based on what is fair and just rather than on legal principles is called equity.	true	false	5.______
6. Even though society changes, law does not change, but remains static.	true	false	6.______
7. Common law refers to decisions by English courts that were based on customs of the people.	true	false	7.______
8. State and federal governments generally determine which actions are criminal and which are not.	true	false	8.______
9. An important concept in our legal system is that the law protects people and at the same time imposes legal duties upon them.	true	false	9.______
10. A person harmed because of a violation of civil law by another person may sue that person and ask for money damages for any harm caused.	true	false	10.______

PART 2: For each statement, write the letter of the best answer in the Answers column.

	ANSWERS	SCORE
1. Unwritten law based on previous court decisions is known as (A) statute law, (B) common law, (C) moral law, (D) constitutional law.	________	1.______
2. In a conflict between laws, the law that takes precedence over all others is (A) constitutional law, (B) common law, (C) statute law, (D) criminal law.	________	2.______
3. Laws passed by cities, towns, and villages are referred to as (A) decrees, (B) ordinances, (C) acts, (D) moral laws.	________	3.______
4. The body of written law that outlines the basic principles that govern a group and forms the basis of a government's power and authority is known as (A) business law, (B) common law, (C) constitutional law, (D) ordinances.	________	4.______
5. Laws enacted by legislative bodies that protect society from the harmful acts of individuals and that impose fines or imprisonment for violations are referred to as (A) moral laws, (B) civil laws, (C) natural laws, (D) criminal laws.	________	5.______
6. Laws that protect the rights and property of individuals from harm by other individuals and that provide remedies for any harm caused are called (A) civil laws, (B) criminal laws, (C) constitutional laws, (D) administrative laws.	________	6.______
7. The main reason rules or laws were first established was to (A) provide jobs for people, (B) restrict people's movement in society, (C) make majority rule possible, (D) protect individual rights against acts by others.	________	7.______
8. Tate maliciously broke into her neighbor's house. Tate's action is governed by (A) criminal law, (B) natural law, (C) equity law, (D) administrative law.	________	8.______

	ANSWERS	SCORE
9. After common law is revised and adopted by a state legislature, it is known as (A) administrative law, (B) commercial law, (C) federal law, (D) statute law.	______	9. ______
10. The Social Security Act is an example of a (A) local ordinance, (B) state statute, (C) federal act, (D) constitutional amendment.	______	10. ______
11. A Federal Communications Commission restriction on cigarette advertising on television is an example of (A) administrative law, (B) constitutional law, (C) criminal law, (D) statute law.	______	11. ______
12. The first kind of law, other than Roman law, to come into existence was (A) constitutional law, (B) administrative law, (C) statute law, (D) common law.	______	12. ______
13. The type of action indicated by the case title *William Beebe v. Katherine Coyle* is (A) civil, (B) criminal, (C) punitive, (D) bankruptcy.	______	13. ______
14. A person who violates criminal law is subject to (A) punishment, (B) a ruling in equity, (C) *stare decisis,* (D) a moral action in a court of law.	______	14. ______
15. In law, *equity* means (A) fair and just, (B) "to stand by a decision," (C) violation of the law, (D) precedent.	______	15. ______

PART 3: Answer each of the following questions in the space provided. SCORE

1. List and describe the four sources of law in the United States.

____

____

____

____

____

____

____ 1. ______

2. Discuss the significance of the *stare decisis* concept.

____

____

____

____ 2. ______

3. Law is constantly changing to reflect the needs and concerns of the people governed by that law. List five changes in the law over the past several years that reflect changes in people's needs.

____

____

____

____ 3. ______

UNIT 1 LAW IN ACTION

Chapter 2 The Legal System of the United States

NAME________________________________ DATE__________

SCORE__________

Study Guide and Review

PART 1: Indicate whether each statement below is true or false by circling either "true" or "false" in the Answers column.

	ANSWERS		*SCORE*
1. "Separation of powers" is a concept that includes both the federal government and state governments.	true	false	1.______
2. Courts sometimes make laws as well as interpret them.	true	false	2.______
3. Any law, whether enacted by Congress or a state legislature, may be declared invalid if it violates the principles of the U.S. Constitution.	true	false	3.______
4. As practiced in the United States, law is simply a matter of right versus wrong.	true	false	4.______
5. The Bill of Rights guarantees each citizen the right to own property.	true	false	5.______
6. Courts do not have the power to give purely advisory opinions.	true	false	6.______
7. Requirements for citizenship are found in the U.S. Constitution.	true	false	7.______
8. Citizenship may only be granted to someone who is born in the United States or whose parents were born in the United States.	true	false	8.______
9. A person born in the United States can never be deprived of citizenship.	true	false	9.______
10. A U.S. citizen may be required to serve in the armed forces.	true	false	10.______

PART 2: For each statement, write the letter of the best answer in the Answers column.

	ANSWERS	*SCORE*
1. The power of a court to hear a case is known as (A) certiorari, (B) venue, (C) jurisdiction, (D) none of these answers.	________	1.______
2. A court that has the power to hear almost any case brought before it is considered to have (A) appellate jurisdiction, (B) constitutional jurisdiction, (C) limited jurisdiction, (D) general jurisdiction.	________	2.______
3. The U.S. Supreme Court's jurisdiction is (A) appellate only, (B) original only, (C) appellate and original, (D) unlimited.	________	3.______
4. The most common means of bringing an appeal before the U.S. Supreme Court is called (A) case, (B) certification, (C) centaurus, (D) certiorari.	________	4.______
5. The major trial courts of the federal court system are called (A) circuit courts, (B) district courts, (C) claims courts, (D) courts of appeal.	________	5.______
6. A court of original jurisdiction is called a (A) trial court, (B) higher court, (C) review court, (D) criminal court only.	________	6.______
7. Appellate courts are courts (A) of original jurisdiction, (B) that hear appeals of lower court decisions, (C) that try only criminal cases, (D) that try only civil cases.	________	7.______
8. The U.S. Supreme Court derives its judicial power from (A) the Congress, (B) the President, (C) the Constitution, (D) state courts.	________	8.______
9. Howell, a landlord, was involved in a dispute with a tenant over unpaid rent. Howell should bring suit against the tenant in (A) district court, (B) Tax Court, (C) probate court, (D) small claims court.	________	9.______
10. Another name for a lawsuit or legal action is (A) certiorari, (B) execution, (C) litigation, (D) jurisdiction.	________	10.______

PART 3: Answer the following questions in the space provided. SCORE

1. Briefly explain the meaning of the following statement: Our legal system is known as an adversary system.

____

____

____

____

____

____

____ 1.______

2. The United States system of government and law is determined by the doctrine of separation of powers. Explain the meaning of this doctrine.

____

____

____

____

____

____

____

____ 2.______

3. Explain why the concept of judicial review is important in our judicial system.

____

____

____

____

____

____

____

____

____ 3.______

NAME ______________________________ DATE ______________

4. What is the main difference between a court with general jurisdiction and a court with limited jurisdiction? *SCORE*

____

____

____

____

______________________________ 4. ______

5. List five responsibilities that U.S. citizens have.

____

____

____

______________________________ 5. ______

PART 4: Read the case problems below and then answer the questions that follow. *SCORE*

Johnson refused to file a federal income tax return, claiming that it was a violation of his right to privacy. He was arrested and charged with a violation of the Internal Revenue Code of the United States.

1. Is this a state or a federal case? ______________________________ 1. ______

2. Which court has jurisdiction to hear this case? ______________________________ 2. ______

3. If Johnson is convicted, to which court may he appeal? ______________________________ 3. ______

Alden had her car radiator repaired by Smokey Garage for $125. She was not happy with the results and decided to sue the garage owner to get her money back.

1. In what court would her case most likely be heard? ______________________________ 1. ______

2. Would she need a lawyer to represent her in this court? ______________________________ 2. ______

3. Would this case normally be heard by a judge or by a jury? ______________________________ 3. ______

Boulder got into a fight with Smyth and fractured Smyth's jaw. Smyth sued Boulder for his injuries.

1. Would this case be tried in a civil or a criminal court? ______________________________ 1. ______

2. Is this a state or a federal case? ______________________________ 2. ______

3. Would this case be heard in a trial or an appellate court? ______________________________ 3. ______

PART 5: Read the problem below and then answer the questions that follow. Explain your answers.

SCORE

Sam Chutter, a naturalized American citizen, received a notice to report for jury duty. Chutter refused to serve on the jury, claiming (1) that only natural-born citizens are required to serve on juries and (2) a citizen is free to decide whether to perform jury service.

1. Is there an obligation to serve on a jury? ______________________________

   ______________________________ 1.______

2. Does the obligation to serve on a jury differ depending on whether a person is a natural-born or a naturalized citizen?

   ______________________________ 2.______

3. Would Chutter be free to refuse to serve on a jury if he were not a citizen?

   ______________________________ 3.______

4. Could Chutter lose his citizenship for refusing to serve?

   ______________________________ 4.______

Activity—Word Search

The 10 words listed below describe important parts of the legal system in the United States. These words can be found in the word search puzzle below. The words read forward, backward, up, down, and diagonally, but always in a straight line and never skipping letters. Circle each word you find.

SCORE

G	L	E	S	T	A	Y	R	O	X	T	Z	B
N	O	I	T	A	G	I	T	I	L	H	R	V
O	O	J	S	T	F	O	C	O	U	R	T	S
I	P	I	H	S	N	E	Z	I	T	I	C	Z
T	A	T	T	O	R	N	E	Y	Z	J	S	Y
C	R	S	G	U	L	F	L	O	E	X	N	R
I	M	I	N	E	T	A	L	L	E	P	P	A
D	K	T	A	G	L	I	T	R	A	I	L	S
S	Y	T	A	L	C	O	T	N	R	N	M	R
I	O	Q	M	W	P	M	L	S	W	L	N	E
R	O	I	T	C	I	D	S	I	N	U	J	V
U	S	E	D	O	P	M	L	O	X	O	C	D
J	S	T	H	G	I	R	L	I	V	I	C	A

adversary
appellate
attorney
citizenship
civil rights
constitution
courts
jurisdiction
litigation
trial

______

UNIT 1 LAW IN ACTION

Chapter 3 Crimes and the Criminal Justice System

NAME________________________________ DATE____________

SCORE____________

Study Guide and Review

PART 1: Indicate whether each statement below is true or false by circling either "true" or "false" in the Answers column.

	ANSWERS		*SCORE*
1. The U.S. criminal justice system is composed of three elements: police, courts, and corrections.	true	false	1.______
2. The punishment for committing a felony could be imprisonment for more than one year.	true	false	2.______
3. Shoplifting is a form of burglary that takes place in a store.	true	false	3.______
4. A person must be formally charged with committing a crime before the person can be tried for that crime.	true	false	4.______
5. A defendant's prior criminal record may affect the punishment given for a crime committed by that person.	true	false	5.______
6. A crime is an act against society that is punishable by law.	true	false	6.______
7. An indictment is a charge by a grand jury that a certain person has committed a felony.	true	false	7.______
8. A misdemeanor is an act punishable by imprisonment for more than one year.	true	false	8.______
9. Two people who are accused of committing the same crime could be treated differently under the law.	true	false	9.______
10. A person guilty of a petty offense will have a permanent criminal record.	true	false	10.______

PART 2: Answer the following questions in the space provided. *SCORE*

1. A person suspected of committing a crime is dealt with through the criminal justice system. Describe the process this person must go through.

____

____

____

____ 1.______

2. List three rights and three defenses a person has after being arrested on suspicion of having committed a crime.

Rights:	Defenses:
____________________	____________________
____________________	____________________
____________________	____________________

2.______

PART 3: For each situation described below, identify the crime or crimes committed by the person underlined. SCORE

1. A fuel-truck driver was charged with skimming more than 100,000 gallons from gasoline deliveries to government agencies and then selling the fuel at cut-rate prices.

______________________________ 1.______

2. A rock band member, tired of having obscenities yelled at him by another band member, struck the other band member over the head with the base of his microphone stand, causing permanent brain damage.

______________________________ 2.______

3. Higgins was charged with entering the Larder residence and taking a handgun, jewelry, coins, and bonds valued at over $1500.

______________________________ 3.______

4. Johnson did not pay her cable TV bill, and her service was cut off. She then ran her own wire to the cable TV company's connection box and received free service.

______________________________ 4.______

5. An escaped prisoner entered a Conway Ice Cream store, pointed a gun at the clerk, and demanded all the money in the cash register.

______________________________ 5.______

6. Driscoll, a store manager, filled out and signed time cards for non-existent employees and then cashed the paychecks himself.

______________________________ 6.______

7. Bonano spray-painted several school buses and let the air out of the tires. ______________

______________________________ 7.______

8. LeBlanc went into a store, put a sweater on, and walked out without paying. ______________

______________________________ 8.______

PART 4: For each statement, write the letter of the best answer in the Answers column. ANSWERS SCORE

1. McCurdy's Department Store delivered merchandise to Mrs. Willis by mistake. Although she knew the merchandise was not hers, she kept it. Mrs. Willis is guilty of (A) nothing, (B) larceny, (C) burglary, (D) robbery. ______ 1.______
2. Weinberg was walking into the South Town Mall when he was attacked. Morrow, the attacker, knocked him down and took his wallet containing $50. Weinberg was seriously injured. Morrow was apprehended by police and charged with (A) assault and burglary, (B) assault and robbery, (C) burglary and robbery, (D) robbery and criminal mischief. ______ 2.______
3. Barnum, bookkeeper for Time Wise Food Wholesalers, made false entries in the company books so that she could take the company's money for her own use. In taking the money, Barnum was guilty of (A) fraud, (B) larceny, (C) robbery, (D) embezzlement. ______ 3.______
4. A felony is a serious crime punishable (A) by a jail sentence of no more than one year, (B) by imprisonment for more than one year, (C) only by death, (D) by a minimum of 5 years' imprisonment. ______ 4.______

NAME ______________________________ DATE ______________

PART 5: Read the following case and then answer the questions that follow. *SCORE*

FACTS: Three police officers went to the home of Chimel in Santa Ana, California, with a warrant for his arrest for a coin store burglary. When they arrived, the officers identified themselves and asked to enter the house. Chimel's wife let them in. When Chimel arrived, the officers arrested him and searched him and the immediate area. Although they did not have a search warrant and Chimel objected, the police then searched the entire house. In the course of this search, they seized a number of coins suspected of being from the coin shop burglary. In a lower court, Chimel was convicted of the burglary based on the introduction of the coins as evidence. He appealed his case to the U.S. Supreme Court on the grounds that the officers' search, without a warrant, of the entire house was unlawful.

SUPREME COURT DECISION: The Fourth Amendment prohibits ''unreasonable searches and seizures'' by government agents. Here, since the arrest was lawful, the Supreme Court found that a search of the arrested person and the ''area of immediate control'' was justified. However, the Court could find no justification for the warrantless search of the entire house. In the Court's interpretation of the Fourth Amendment, police officers are required to obtain a search warrant from a court before conducting a search unless some special circumstance justifies a warrantless search. In this case, the Court found no special circumstances concerning the search of the entire house. Therefore, the Court held that such a search should have been limited to the area where the arrest occurred. Otherwise, a warrant should have been obtained in order to search the entire house. (Chimel v. California, 395 U.S. 752)

1. Identify and define the crime involved in this case. ______________________________

______________________________ 1. ______

2. Briefly summarize the facts in this case. ______________________________

____

______________________________ 2. ______

3. What was the lower court's decision? ______________________________

______________________________ 3. ______

4. What was the Supreme Court's decision regarding the officers' search of Chimel and of the entire house?

____

____

______________________________ 4. ______

5. Do you agree with the Supreme Court's findings? Why or why not? ______________________________

____

____

______________________________ 5. ______

PART 6: For each of the following case problems, give a decision by writing ''yes'' or ''no'' in the space provided. Then, in sentence form, give a reason for your decision. SCORE

1. At 3 a.m., Benton entered a store through an unlocked window. He gathered several valuable items, intending to steal them. When he heard the police coming, he left everything there and was caught by the police as he climbed out the window. Can Benton be charged with burglary even though he took nothing?

Decision: ______________________________

Reason: ______________________________

____

______________________________ 1. ______

2. You bought a set of high-quality stereo speakers for $50 from someone selling them from the back of a van. The police stopped you several blocks away and arrested you for possession of stolen property. Can you claim in defense that you are not guilty because you did not know the speakers were stolen?

Decision: ______________________________

Reason: ______________________________

____

____

______________________________ 2. ______

Activity—Word Puzzle

Make as many words as you can by moving from one diamond to another. The words are names of crimes discussed in this chapter. You may move up, down, or diagonally as long as you move only to an adjoining letter. You may not skip a letter.

F

F I

T I L

I N Y O

M E R P B

B C G R O B

E U R A S N E

Z A L Y H R

Z O R T Y

L F N S

E E E

M M

T

____

____

____

____

____

____

____

SCORE ______

UNIT 1 LAW IN ACTION

Chapter 4 Torts and the Civil Justice System

NAME____________________ DATE__________

SCORE__________

Study Guide and Review

PART 1: Identify the tort in each of the following cases.

	ANSWERS	SCORE
1. At Elmwood General Hospital, an 81-year-old patient died after a nurse accidentally gave him a toxic liquid instead of his medication.	____________	1.______
2. A 21-year-old student was paralyzed from the neck down when a poorly maintained platform collapsed at Wonder Amusement Park.	____________	2.______
3. A surgeon performing eye surgery failed to follow standard post-operative procedure in measuring and minimizing pressure on the eye. As a result, the 7-year-old patient lost sight in one eye.	____________	3.______
4. Neighbors complained that Huber's property was "a junkyard and a breeding ground for rodents." County health investigators confirmed that the property was "a source of filth and a health hazard that affected the entire neighborhood."	____________	4.______
5. Because of poor management practices in his department, a high-level hospital staff member was being investigated. Hospital officials searched his desk, including personal papers and belongings, while he was at lunch. As a result of this search, they discovered that he had once been under psychiatric care.	____________	5.______

PART 2: Read the following case and answer the questions that follow. *SCORE*

Wilson entered into a contract with Marple to paint Marple's house for $900. When Wilson completed the job, Marple refused to pay, claiming the work was not done properly, the wrong paint was used, and the job was not finished on time. Wilson brought suit against Marple to collect the amount due.

1. Who is the plaintiff? ____________________ 1.______

2. Who is the defendant? ____________________ 2.______

3. What are the two documents Wilson will use to start his suit against Marple? ____________

____________________ 3.______

4. If Marple wishes to raise the defense that the work was performed improperly, in what legal document will he state this defense?

____________________ 4.______

5. If Wilson wishes to learn why Marple was dissatisfied with the job, what type of proceedings can he use?

____________________ 5.______

PART 3: Write the letter of the best answer in the Answers column.

	ANSWERS	SCORE
1. The main difference between libel and slander is (A) libel concerns adults only; slander, minors only, (B) libel concerns minors only; slander, adults only, (C) libel concerns those things spoken; slander, those things in print, (D) libel concerns those things in print; slander, those things spoken.	______	1.______
2. The purpose of a summons is to (A) notify the defendant of a lawsuit, (B) inform a juror of his or her duty to serve on a case, (C) inform the attorneys of the time and date a trial is to begin, (D) notify a witness to appear in court.	______	2.______
3. An arbitrator's decision is known as (A) a dispute, (B) mediation, (C) an award, (D) money damages.	______	3.______
4. Two examples of torts are (A) arson and embezzlement, (B) robbery and forgery, (C) nuisance and negligence, (D) burglary and extortion.	______	4.______
5. Martin, a bill collector, was kicked and punched by Beaden while trying to collect an overdue account from Beaden. Beaden could be held for his tort of (A) libel, (B) embezzlement, (C) extortion, (D) assault and battery.	______	5.______
6. The parties involved in a civil lawsuit are known as the (A) plaintiff and the state, (B) plaintiff and the defendant, (C) defendant and the state, (D) defendant and the public defender.	______	6.______
7. By orally repeating a rumor she knew to be false, Marny damaged Jewell's reputation. Marny was guilty of (A) trespass, (B) libel, (C) assault, (D) slander.	______	7.______
8. The people selected to determine the disputed facts in a civil lawsuit are known as (A) jurors, (B) defendants, (C) witnesses, (D) plaintiffs.	______	8.______
9. Benzer bought a television that, unknown to him, was stolen. Benzer refused to surrender the television until he was reimbursed the money he paid to the seller. Benzer is liable for the tort of (A) fraud, (B) trespass, (C) negligence, (D) conversion.	______	9.______
10. Curtis built a fence on what she thought was the border between her property and her neighbor's. A month later, she found that the fence was on her neighbor's property. The neighbor could hold Curtis liable for (A) nuisance, (B) trespass, (C) a criminal wrong, (D) nothing, because the act was unintentional.	______	10.______
11. Compensatory damages are (A) imposed upon the wrongdoer as a punishment, (B) also called exemplary damages, (C) imposed to cover actual damages such as doctor bills and "pain and suffering," (D) also called nominal damages.	______	11.______
12. Lovell threatened to hit Farrin. If Farrin suffered injury or damages from the threat, she could sue Lovell for (A) nuisance, (B) assault only, (C) battery only, (D) assault and battery.	______	12.______
13. In a civil action, the document containing the defendant's statement of his or her defense is called (A) the summons, (B) the discovery, (C) the answer, (D) direct examination.	______	13.______
14. A person accused of shoplifting was detained in a store for an unreasonable length of time, but a search revealed no evidence of shoplifting. The detained person may sue for the tort of (A) robbery, (B) larceny, (C) false imprisonment, (D) trespass.	______	14.______
15. A surgeon performed an appendectomy on Frank. One month later, Frank discovered that the surgeon had left some gauze in his incision, causing infection, considerable pain, and additional hospital expenses. Frank sued the surgeon to recover money damages. The basis for Frank's lawsuit is (A) nuisance, (B) invasion of privacy, (C) conversion, (D) malpractice.	______	15.______
16. DiBella, a dentist, received a very derogatory letter from a former patient who was not satisfied with DiBella's work. DiBella may sue this patient for (A) libel, (B) slander, (C) conversion, (D) none of these.	______	16.______
17. In court, an application to a judge for a ruling on a point of law is known as a (A) discovery, (B) award, (C) motion, (D) summons.	______	17.______
18. If a case is tried without a jury, the judge considers all the evidence and then gives a decision. This decision by the judge is known as a (A) verdict, (B) judgment, (C) complaint, (D) discovery.	______	18.______

NAME ______________________________ DATE ____________

PART 4: Read the statement below and then answer the questions that follow. SCORE

The torts of false arrest and false imprisonment are often confused. They are similar in some ways and different in others.

1. Explain the difference between false arrest and false imprisonment. ____________________

____

____

____

____

____

____ 1. ______

2. Give a brief example of each. ____________________

____

____

____

____

____

____ 2. ______

PART 5: Rearrange the following events in the order in which they occur: SCORE

summons and complaint	1. ____________
discovery proceedings	2. ____________
attorneys' opening statements	3. ____________
answer	4. ____________
presentation of evidence for the defendant	5. ____________
verdict	6. ____________
presentation of evidence for the plaintiff	7. ____________
attorneys' closing statements	8. ____________
appeal	9. ____________ ______

PART 6: In the space provided, answer the following questions. SCORE

1. What are the differences among litigation (a lawsuit), arbitration, and mediation?

1. ______

2. Explain malicious prosecution. In order to sue for this tort, what must a person show?

2. ______

3. Two common defenses in a lawsuit based on negligence are contributory negligence and comparative negligence. What are the differences between these two defenses?

3. ______

UNIT 1 LAW IN ACTION

Chapter 5 Young People and the Juvenile Justice System

NAME________________________ DATE____________

SCORE____________

Study Guide and Review

PART 1: Indicate whether each statement below is true or false by circling either "true" or "false" in the Answers column.

	ANSWERS		SCORE
1. A minor is a person who has not yet reached the age of majority in his or her state.	true	false	1.______
2. Minors are generally not liable for their own torts.	true	false	2.______
3. A child is emancipated upon reaching adulthood or by becoming self-supporting.	true	false	3.______
4. Parents have the legal duty to support their children and pay for their necessities until the children become emancipated.	true	false	4.______
5. School personnel have no right to search a student or a student's locker under any circumstances.	true	false	5.______
6. Students may express their opinions in school as long as they do not disrupt the education of others.	true	false	6.______
7. A minor who commits an unlawful act is charged with a crime.	true	false	7.______
8. Cases involving juveniles who commit unlawful acts are generally handled in adult courts.	true	false	8.______
9. Schools must submit your school records to anyone seeking information about you.	true	false	9.______
10. Minors do not have any civil rights when they are arrested.	true	false	10.______

PART 2: For each statement, write the letter of the best answer in the Answers column.

	ANSWERS	SCORE
1. Parents are liable for a tort committed by their minor child (A) under any circumstances, (B) only if the child is under 10 years of age, (C) if the parent fails to stop a child from repeating acts about which the parents have been warned, (D) only if the child is between 10 and 15 years of age.	________	1.______
2. When a child continually disobeys parents to the point of being out of control, parents (A) may ask the court to declare the child a PINS, (B) may ask the court to declare the child a juvenile delinquent, (C) have no rights, (D) may have the child jailed.	________	2.______
3. A judge who finds a minor guilty of juvenile delinquency may place the minor (A) in a secured juvenile detention facility if the juvenile's behavior poses a threat to society, (B) under the supervision and custody of parents, (C) in a group home, (D) either A, B, or C, depending upon the seriousness of the act.	________	3.______
4. A juvenile found to be delinquent will have (A) no more rights as a citizen, (B) a record, (C) a suspension hearing in school, (D) all of these answers.	________	4.______
5. If a student is to be given a long-term suspension, the student must (A) accept the punishment without question, (B) be in at least the 12th grade, (C) first consult with her or his teachers, (D) be granted a hearing.	________	5.______
6. A student's freedom of speech (A) is granted by state law, (B) is an absolute right, (C) is granted by the U.S. Constitution, (D) does not apply to all schools.	________	6.______
7. Controversial speech in schools (A) can be prohibited by administrators in order to maintain a calm atmosphere, (B) is allowed only in school assemblies, (C) is allowed only in social studies classes, (D) can be restricted if there is substantial disruption of the educational process.	________	7.______

ANSWERS SCORE

8. Wearing armbands, buttons, and other symbols (A) is protected the same as actual speech, (B) is symbolic speech and is therefore protected, (C) can be restricted if it causes substantial disruption, (D) all of these answers. ________ 8.______
9. Administrators may search school lockers (A) only if the lockers are assigned or rented, (B) only with search warrants, (C) if they have reason to suspect illegal or dangerous things are in a locker, (D) only if teachers request a search. ________ 9.______
10. School officials (A) may never do a "body search," (B) may do a "body search" only with a search warrant, (C) may do "body searches" only if police are present, (D) none of these answers. ________ 10.______

PART 3: In the Answers column, write the word or words that best complete each statement.

ANSWERS SCORE

Example: A minor is a person below a certain age set by state ______. law

1. School officials may legally search students or their lockers when there is reasonable ______ of a crime that threatens the safety and welfare of the student body. ________ 1.______
2. Before school authorities may discipline a student for violating a school rule, the student is entitled to ______ ______ under the Fourteenth Amendment. ________ 2.______
3. If a student is to be given a long-term suspension (generally in excess of five days), the opportunity for a ______ must be granted. ________ 3.______
4. Under the Family Educational Rights and Privacy Act, parents or legal guardians of students under 18 years of age are given the right to inspect the students' ______. ________ 4.______
5. School authorities cannot use interference with academic progress, such as arbitrarily lowering a grade, as a means to ______ students. ________ 5.______

Activity—What's Your Opinion?

In the space provided, state whether you agree or disagree with each statement. Support your position in each case.

SCORE

1. Juveniles accused of a crime should be treated the same as adults.

____
____
____
____
____ 1.______

2. School officials should be allowed to conduct random drug tests of students at their schools.

____
____
____
____
____ 2.______

NAME ____ DATE ______________

PART 4: Read the following newspaper story and then answer the questions that follow. *SCORE*

TWO TEENS ACCUSED OF DESTROYING HEADSTONES

Two 15-year-old Rochester boys were charged with destroying about 170 headstones at Holy Sepulchre Cemetery on Lake Avenue, according to Detective Ron Haber of the Rochester Police Department. The boys were caught after an unidentified caller contacted police after overhearing the boys talking about the incident. Because of their ages, the boys' names were not released. Haber estimated damages at $10,000. The two boys were taken into custody and taken to the Lake Avenue Police Station. They were later released to their parents pending possible juvenile court action. About 60 headstones in the cemetery's Grand Army of the Republic Civil War section were among those toppled, Haber said. Because of the age of some of the graves, there may be some difficulty matching tombstones with some graves, according to cemetery officials.

1. What adult crime have the boys committed? ______________________ 1. ______

2. Did taking the boys into custody constitute an arrest? ______________________

______________________ 2. ______

3. Since they are not old enough to be treated as adult criminal offenders, what will they be charged with?

______________________ 3. ______

4. What are the options for handling this case? ______________________

____

____

____

____

______________________ 4. ______

5. What option would you recommend? Why? ______________________

____

____

______________________ 5. ______

6. Under what circumstances will the boys have a criminal record? ______________________

____

____

____

______________________ 6. ______

Activity—Case Analysis

Read the following case and then answer the questions that follow.

SCORE

John Tinker, 15, his sister Mary Beth, 13, and Christopher Eckhardt, 16, were students in Des Moines, Iowa. In December 1965, they joined a group opposed to the Vietnam War. Members of this group planned to express their opposition to the war by wearing black armbands during the holidays. John, Mary Beth, and Christopher decided to participate.

When Des Moines school officials learned of the plan to wear armbands, they adopted a policy stating that students wearing armbands would be asked to remove them. Students who refused would be suspended and sent home until they agreed not to wear the armbands. This policy was announced to all students.

On December 16, the three students wore black armbands to school. They were suspended and sent home. Charging that their right to freedom of expression had been violated, the students sought an injunction in District Court prohibiting their suspensions. At a hearing held to determine whether such an injunction was warranted, the students' lawyer argued that the school was restricting the students' free expression of their opposition to the Vietnam War. The lawyer also revealed that in the past students had been permitted to wear ordinary political buttons and other emblems.

1. Is wearing an armband in school a form of expression protected by the First Amendment? Why or why not?

____

____

______________________________ 1. ______

2. If one of the protesting students made a speech against the Vietnam War in the middle of math class, is that student protected by the First Amendment? Explain.

____

____

______________________________ 2. ______

3. How would your decision be affected if the school had adopted a policy ten years ago that prohibited the wearing of armbands or other items not related to school activities?

____

____

______________________________ 3. ______

4. How would your decision be affected if students supporting the Vietnam War caused a disruption in school because the protesting students wore armbands?

____

____

______________________________ 4. ______

UNIT 1 LAW IN ACTION

Review

NAME______________________________ DATE__________

SCORE__________

Review

PART 1: Indicate whether each statement below is true by circling either "true" or "false" in the Answers column.

	ANSWERS		*SCORE*
1. An important principle of the U.S. legal system is separation of powers.	true	false	1.______
2. In a criminal case, the state or the federal government represents society against the individual accused of the crime.	true	false	2.______
3. Laws passed by Congress and by state legislatures are called common laws.	true	false	3.______
4. Any law enacted by a state legislature or municipality that conflicts with that state's constitution may be declared invalid by a court of law.	true	false	4.______
5. A federal court decision may always be appealed to the U.S. Supreme Court.	true	false	5.______
6. The primary difference between a felony and a misdemeanor is the seriousness of the act committed.	true	false	6.______
7. Most serious crimes are usually punishable by a sentence of a year or more in a state or federal prison.	true	false	7.______
8. A judge who finds a juvenile guilty of breaking the law has the option of placing the juvenile on probation.	true	false	8.______
9. School personnel may search a student's locker when there is reasonable suspicion that the student is involved in criminal activity.	true	false	9.______
10. Generally, parents are liable for the torts of their children.	true	false	10.______
11. Compensatory damages are imposed upon a wrongdoer by the court as punishment for an intentional tort.	true	false	11.______
12. A student can be suspended for unlawful conduct or activities that occur off school grounds.	true	false	12.______
13. In most states, a minor must have a work permit before beginning a job.	true	false	13.______
14. All persons taken into police custody have the right of due process.	true	false	14.______
15. An important consideration in determining a minor's liability for both torts and crimes is the minor's age.	true	false	15.______

PART 2: For each statement, write the letter of the best answer in the Answers column.

	ANSWERS	*SCORE*
1. The function of the grand jury is (A) to prosecute the defendant, (B) to judge the defendant guilty or not guilty of the charges, (C) to decide whether there is sufficient evidence to bring a case to trial, (D) to prove to the court that the defendant is guilty as charged.	________	1.______
2. Once a case has been brought to trial, the first court procedure in a lawsuit is (A) jury selection, (B) the jury's verdict, (C) the attorneys' opening statements to the jury, (D) the judge's charge to the jury.	________	2.______
3. While playing football in an empty lot, Mark hit a passerby in the eye with the ball. This is an example of (A) a felony, (B) a tort, (C) a misdemeanor, (D) an infraction.	________	3.______
4. Libel and slander are considered to be forms of (A) negligence, (B) conspiracy, (C) fraud, (D) defamation.	________	4.______

	ANSWERS	SCORE
5. Refusal to return to its rightful owner stolen property that you purchased is a tort known as (A) attachment, (B) trespass, (C) conversion, (D) specific performance.	________	5. ______
6. Blain's neighbor charged him with assault and battery. Blain was handed a legal notice directing him to appear in court to answer the charges. This notice is known as (A) an answer, (B) a subpoena, (C) a summons, (D) none of these answers.	________	6. ______
7. Potter won her negligence lawsuit against Mann. The $100,000 awarded to Potter is known as the (A) judgment, (B) sentence, (C) indictment, (D) injunction.	________	7. ______
8. Marcella leaves her garbage outside in an uncovered barrel. Because the resulting bad smell bothers the neighbors, this is an example of (A) fraud, (B) trespass, (C) nuisance, (D) conversion.	________	8. ______
9. The person who initiates a civil action is known as the (A) defendant, (B) plaintiff, (C) state, (D) district attorney.	________	9. ______
10. A grand jury has the authority to issue (A) a judgment, (B) an indictment, (C) a verdict, (D) an award.	________	10. ______
11. An example of an act classified as a crime is (A) arson, (B) nuisance, (C) slander, (D) invasion of privacy.	________	11. ______
12. An example of a valid defense that the defendant's attorney may introduce during a criminal trial is (A) the defendant did not know the act was wrong, (B) entrapment, (C) the defendant was instructed to perform the illegal act as a joke, (D) the defendant committed the act out of necessity.	________	12. ______
13. *United States v. Powers* is an example of a case title indicating (A) a state civil case, (B) a state criminal case, (C) a federal civil case, (D) a federal criminal case.	________	13. ______
14. Common law is often referred to as (A) written law, (B) administrative law, (C) equity law, (D) unwritten law.	________	14. ______
15. A judge's practice of following the precedents established by past decisions is called (A) equity, (B) indictment, (C) *stare decisis,* (D) an act of Congress.	________	15. ______
16. If Bartel dumped trash on Frank's land, Bartel could be held liable for (A) fraud, (B) negligence, (C) conversion, (D) trespass.	________	16. ______
17. Taking money that belongs to someone else and that has been given to you for safekeeping is the crime of (A) embezzlement, (B) robbery, (C) forgery, (D) arson.	________	17. ______
18. The questioning of a plaintiff's witness by the defendant's attorney is known as (A) direct examination, (B) indictment, (C) cross-examination, (D) objection.	________	18. ______
19. An effort to make laws similar among states has been attempted through (A) the Uniform Commercial Code, (B) an amendment to the state constitutions, (C) an amendment to the U.S. Constitution, (D) local ordinances within each state.	________	19. ______
20. Common law is a system of law that developed (A) after the 18th century, (B) after the United States was founded, (C) in the early American colonies, (D) in England, with precedents established from prior disputes.	________	20. ______
21. Punitive damages are awarded to someone injured by another person's intentional tort (A) so the injured party can make a profit, (B) so the injured party is compensated for hospital and doctor bills, (C) to punish the party who committed the tort, (D) so the person committing the tort can make a profit.	________	21. ______
22. When Bond's apartment lease ended, her landlord inspected the apartment and found no damage beyond ordinary wear and tear. The landlord promised to return her $300 security deposit within a week, but several months later, Bond was still trying to get her money. To get an inexpensive, quick, fair settlement, Bond should (A) ask the public defender to represent her at state expense in a town justice court, (B) take her case to small claims court, (C) take her case to the highest state court, (D) obtain a writ of execution to seize and sell the landlord's property.	________	22. ______
23. Carmel struck a legally parked car while backing carelessly out of his driveway. Carmel could be found guilty of the tort of (A) nuisance, (B) negligence, (C) assault and battery, (D) conversion.	________	23. ______
24. A body of law that states the rights and limitations of both the federal government and of state governments is classified as (A) administrative, (B) constitutional, (C) common, (D) statutory.	________	24. ______

NAME____ DATE______________

ANSWERS SCORE

25. A convicted criminal claimed that his constitutional rights had been violated. The highest court that can pass judgment on his claim is the (A) highest state court, (B) U.S. Court of Claims, (C) Federal District Court, (D) U.S. Supreme Court. ________ 25.______
26. Laws enacted by legislative bodies that forbid conduct harmful to society and that impose fines or imprisonment for violations are referred to as (A) moral laws, (B) civil laws, (C) natural laws, (D) criminal laws. ________ 26.______
27. In the United States, law is derived from (A) written laws, such as constitutions, statutes, and ordinances, (B) case law, which is based on judicial decisions, (C) administrative agencies' rules and regulations, (D) all of these answers. ________ 27.______
28. If Keith breaks into Pick's house while Pick is away and steals a painting, Keith may be found guilty of the crimes of (A) burglary and robbery, (B) arson and misrepresentation, (C) burglary and larceny, (D) arson and larceny. ________ 28.______
29. A person who suffers mentally as a result of another person's extreme conduct may sue for (A) battery, (B) conversion, (C) emotional distress, (D) trespass. ________ 29.______
30. Detaining a person in a restaurant to see whether the bill has been paid would be considered (A) a battery, (B) a nuisance, (C) a trespass, (D) false imprisonment. ________ 30.______
31. The relief granted in a civil action is (A) punishment, (B) confinement in a state prison, (C) confinement in a county jail, (D) money damages. ________ 31.______
32. A court of original jurisdiction is called (A) a trial court, (B) a higher court, (C) a review court, (D) a criminal court only. ________ 32.______
33. By law, since parents are providing support for their minor children, they are entitled to the children's (A) education, (B) earnings, (C) privileges, (D) torts. ________ 33.______
34. The Family Educational Rights and Privacy Act gives students and their parents the right to (A) express their opinions in school, (B) file a PINS petition in juvenile court, (C) inspect school records and challenge inaccurate, misleading, or inappropriate entries, (D) all of these answers. ________ 34.______
35. An act of habitual misbehavior other than a crime is a (A) PINS, (B) juvenile delinquent, (C) sanction, (D) status offense. ________ 35.______

PART 3: In the Answers column at the right, write the word or words that make each statement correct.

ANSWERS SCORE

1. A court decision that has the force of law is a _______. ________________ 1.______
2. A serious violation of a school rule may result in _______. ________________ 2.______
3. Shoplifting is usually considered a _______. ________________ 3.______
4. A court that has the power to hear any case brought before it has _______ jurisdiction. ________________ 4.______
5. An important consideration in determining a minor's liability for both torts and crimes is the minor's _______. ________________ 5.______
6. A person who violates a criminal law is subject to _______. ________________ 6.______
7. Rights that allow citizens to participate in the process of government are _______ rights. ________________ 7.______
8. A trial court's jurisdiction is _______. ________________ 8.______
9. All persons who are taken into custody by the police have the right of _______. ________________ 9.______
10. Personal rights and freedoms guaranteed by the U.S. Constitution and the state constitutions are _______. ________________ 10.______

Application Practice

In the space provided below, write a paragraph of about 200 words explaining why it is important for you to understand the law and how it works.

SCORE

UNIT 2 CONTRACTS

Chapter 6 Basic Contract Law

NAME______________________________ DATE____________

SCORE____________

Study Guide and Review

PART 1: For each statement, write the letter of the best answer in the Answers column.

	ANSWERS	SCORE
1. Oral contracts (A) are not legal, (B) cannot be enforced in court, (C) lack agreement, (D) are harder to prove than written contracts.	______	1.______
2. An illegal contract would generally be considered (A) valid, (B) voidable, (C) implied, (D) void.	______	2.______
3. Karla fully performed her part of a contract to the complete satisfaction of Briggs, who has not yet paid Karla. This is an example of (A) an executory contract, (B) an executed contract, (C) a formal contract, (D) a void contract.	______	3.______
4. Contracts that involve important or complicated matters should be (A) implied in fact, (B) written, (C) breached, (D) implied in law.	______	4.______
5. If either party fails to perform her or his duties under the terms of a contract, the contract has been (A) performed, (B) breached, (C) enforced, (D) executed.	______	5.______
6. Another name for a contract implied in law is (A) an executed contract, (B) a written contract, (C) a quasi-contract, (D) an express contract.	______	6.______
7. Bart agreed to sell Sean his motorcycle for $900. Sean paid Bart $900, and Bart promised delivery the next day. This is an example of (A) an implied contract, (B) an executed contract, (C) an executory contract, (D) a void contract.	______	7.______
8. For a contract to be valid, four essential elements are required. Which of the following is *not* an essential element of a valid contract: (A) offer and acceptance, (B) competent parties, (C) consideration, (D) written form.	______	8.______
9. Peter promised to pay Carter $25 if he repaired a lawnmower. Carter repaired the lawnmower, but has not yet been paid. At this point, this contract is (A) valid, unilateral, and executory, (B) valid, bilateral, and executory, (C) valid, bilateral, and executed, (D) valid, unilateral, and executed.	______	9.______
10. To create a legally binding contract, both parties to the agreement must be (A) able to read and write, (B) able to speak and understand English, (C) financially responsible, (D) competent.	______	10.______
11. A bilateral contract involves (A) an act for an act, (B) an act for a promise, (C) a promise for a promise, (D) a promise for an act.	______	11.______
12. Bentley, a minor, bought a set of golf clubs for $89.95 from Mickey's Sporting Goods Shop. This is an example of a (A) void contract, (B) voidable contract, (C) quasi-contract, (D) social agreement.	______	12.______
13. A contract implied in fact (A) does not exist in the eyes of the law, (B) is expressed orally or in writing, (C) arises from the actions of the parties rather than from a specific agreement, (D) will not generally be enforced by a court because competent parties are lacking.	______	13.______
14. An express contract is one in which (A) no specific oral or written agreement is made, (B) the agreement is specifically stated, (C) neither party can enforce the contract against the other in court, (D) no legal obligation is intended.	______	14.______
15. A contract that will be enforced unless a party legally entitled to avoid the contract does so is called a (A) void contract, (B) voidable contract, (C) quasi-contract, (D) contract implied in law.	______	15.______

PART 2: For each of the following case problems, give a decision by writing "yes" or "no." Then, in sentence form, give a reason for your decision.

SCORE

1. Armond and his girlfriend went to the movies. Without saying anything, Armond handed the ticket seller $10. The ticket seller, also without speaking, handed Armond two tickets. Was any type of contract formed?

Decision: ______________________________

Reason: ______________________________

____

______________________________ 1. ______

2. Berger fainted at a shopping mall. A security guard arranged with police to have her taken to a hospital for emergency treatment. When she regained consciousness and was about to be discharged, the business office asked her to sign papers arranging for her insurance company to pay the bill. Berger refused to sign, claiming she had not made any agreement with the hospital for treatment. The hospital sued Berger. Would a court require Berger to pay the bill?

Decision: ______________________________

Reason: ______________________________

____

______________________________ 2. ______

3. Stevens agreed to take his friend Anderson to lunch. He said to Anderson: "Meet me at the Royal Scot Restaurant at 12:30 tomorrow afternoon." Anderson agreed. Stevens never showed up. Does Anderson have a legal claim against Stevens for breach of contract?

Decision: ______________________________

Reason: ______________________________

____

______________________________ 3. ______

4. Mason, who has a degree in Business Administration, interviewed for two positions, one as a credit manager for a large bank and the other as a financial planner. He received a telephone call offering him the credit manager position, which he accepted. Two days later he was offered the financial planner job, his first choice. He also accepted this position and then called the bank to say he had changed his mind about taking the credit manager position. Has Mason breached a contract with the bank?

Decision: ______________________________

Reason: ______________________________

____

______________________________ 4. ______

NAME____ DATE______________

5. The Isaac Heating Company randomly sent out letters to residents of the town where it did business. The letter read: ''Special—We offer to clean your furnace for 50% off our regular price.'' Martell received one of the letters. Did a contract result between Isaac Heating Company and Martell when Martell received the letter? *SCORE*

Decision: ____

Reason: ____

____

____ 5.______

6. Serono agreed to sell her horse to Branston. Unknown to either of them, the horse had been hit by a car and killed. Can either party still enforce the contract in court?

Decision: ____

Reason: ____

____

____ 6.______

PART 3: Read the problem below and then answer the questions that follow. *SCORE*

On January 7 Harry Owens, owner of Custom Cleaners, offered to clean the carpets in James Harrington's law office for $350. Harrington agreed to this offer on January 9. On January 20, Owens cleaned the carpets and was paid $350.

1. Who is the offeror? ____ 1.______
2. Who is the offeree? ____ 2.______
3. When was the offer accepted? ____ 3.______
4. What did each party give as consideration to bind the agreement? ____________________

   ____ 4.______
5. Was the contract executed? ____ 5.______

PART 4: Read the following contract and then list the items that are missing. There are at least four missing items. *SCORE*

This agreement is made between David Richardson and Edward Warren. Richardson agrees to clean and paint the outside surface of Warren's frame dwelling, using paint and materials supplied by Edward Warren, and applying two coats of paint. In consideration of this, Edward Warren agrees to pay David Richardson upon satisfactory completion of the work.

1.____________________ 3.____________________

2.____________________ 4.____________________ ______

PART 5: Answer the following questions in the space provided. SCORE

1. What does the following statement mean: "All contracts are agreements, but not all agreements are contracts."

____

____

____

____

____

____

____

____ 1.______

2. Why should a contract involving an important or complicated matter be written?

____

____

____

____ 2.______

3. Other than money, what forms may consideration take?

____

____

____

____

____ 3.______

4. What is meant by the term "competent parties"?

____

____

____

____

____ 4.______

UNIT 2 CONTRACTS

Chapter 7 Offer and Acceptance

NAME____ DATE____________

SCORE____________

Study Guide and Review

PART 1: For each statement, write the letter of the best answer in the Answers column.

	ANSWERS	*SCORE*
1. The Budget Office Furniture Company advertised a 60″ x 30″ executive desk for $179.59 in its office supplies catalog. Marlow went to the store and told the salesperson that she wanted to buy one of the advertised desks. Marlow's action was (A) an agreement, (B) an acceptance, (C) an offer, (D) a bilateral contract.	______	1.____
2. An example of a valid offer is (A) a notice of a reward for finding a lost dog, (B) an advertisement to sell a car, (C) an offer that is made in jest, (D) an offer to sell a stolen stereo.	______	2.____
3. If no fixed time is stated for an offer to remain open, the offer (A) ends automatically after 30 days, (B) ends after a reasonable time, (C) ends when the offeree states that it is ended, (D) remains open indefinitely.	______	3.____
4. Your friend made the following statement: "I might sell my car next month if I can get a good price." This statement is (A) an offer to a formal contract, (B) an offer to a unilateral contract, (C) an offer to a bilateral contract, (D) not an offer.	______	4.____
5. When goods are sold at an ordinary auction, acceptance takes place when (A) the auctioneer lets the gavel fall, (B) the offeree pays for the goods, (C) the auctioneer accepts a bid from the highest bidder, (D) the auctioneer presents the goods for sale.	______	5.____
6. Carlos bid $125 for an antique table at a flea market auction. This bid is legally considered (A) an acceptance to an offer, (B) a bilateral contract, (C) a counteroffer, (D) a valid offer.	______	6.____
7. Revocation of an offer takes place when (A) the offeror has been properly notified, (B) the offeree has been properly notified, (C) a proper counteroffer is made, (D) the offeree properly refuses the offer.	______	7.____
8. Unless stated otherwise, acceptance of an offer made by mail takes place as soon as the letter of acceptance is (A) written by the offeree, (B) mailed by the offeree, (C) received by the offeror, (D) received by the offeree.	______	8.____
9. Fowler, an antique dealer, wrote a letter to Gorcey on May 9 offering to sell Gorcey the grandfather clock that Gorcey had seen at Fowler's antique show. The letter stated that the acceptance had to be received by May 15. Gorcey mailed a letter of acceptance on May 15 that reached Fowler on May 16. A valid contract was made (A) on May 15, (B) on May 9, (C) on May 16, (D) at no time.	______	9.____
10. If Stornelli pays Mooney $50 to keep an offer for the sale of a personal computer open for a definite length of time, their agreement is called (A) a counteroffer, (B) an option, (C) a breach, (D) a quasi-contract.	______	10.____
11. Preston offered to sell a camera to Bellino, but then withdrew the offer before Bellino could accept. Preston's withdrawal of the offer is known as (A) revocation, (B) an option, (C) a counteroffer, (D) acceptance.	______	11.____

PART 2: For each of the following case problems, give a decision by writing ''yes'' or ''no'' in the space provided. Then, in sentence form, give a reason for your decision.

SCORE

1. Archer, in Chicago, wrote to Ganze in New York City offering to purchase 500 pairs of jogging shoes. When she received the letter, Ganze mailed an acceptance. After she mailed the letter, Ganze changed her mind and sent a telegram rejecting the offer. The telegram and the letter reached Archer at the same time. Did a contract result?

Decision: ________________________________

Reason: ________________________________

____

________________________________ 1.______

2. Jordan said to Beacher, ''I'll sell you my telescope for $60.'' Beacher replied, ''I won't give you $60, but I will give you $45.'' Jordan said no. Beacher then changed his mind and said ''O.K., I'll give you $60.'' Jordan refused to sell the telescope to Beacher, saying it was too late and he had decided to keep it. Beacher is now claiming breach of contract. Did a contract arise between Jordan and Beacher?

Decision: ________________________________

Reason: ________________________________

____

________________________________ 2.______

3. Wurzer subscribed to *Weight Lifters* magazine. About 3 months before the subscription ran out, he received a letter from the publishing company stating that his subscription would be renewed on the renewal date unless he notified the company to the contrary. Wurzer did not reply or renew his subscription. Is Wurzer bound to a contract for the subscription renewal?

Decision: ________________________________

Reason: ________________________________

____

________________________________ 3.______

4. Perez offered a $25 reward for the return of an expensive calculator watch he had lost. Jarvis saw the notice in the newspaper and returned the watch, but Perez refused to give her the reward. Does Jarvis have a legal right to the reward?

Decision: ________________________________

Reason: ________________________________

____

________________________________ 4.______

NAME________________________________ DATE______________

5. Earle offered Grant $450 for her computer printer and told her that she had until noon the following day to accept. At 9 the next morning, Earle called Grant and withdrew his offer. Nevertheless, at 11 a.m. Grant called Earle back and accepted his offer, noting that Earle had given her until noon of that day to accept. Is Grant's acceptance legally binding?

SCORE

Decision: ____

Reason: ____

____

____

____ 5.______

Activity—Case Analysis

Read the case below and then answer the questions that follow.

SCORE

Following the assassination of President Abraham Lincoln on April 14, 1865, by John Wilkes Booth and John H. Surratt, one of Booth's suspected accomplices, the Secretary of War published the following reward offer in various newspapers:

> $25,000 reward to the person who apprehends John H. Surratt and a $10,000 reward for information leading to the arrest of John H. Surratt.

Sometime afterward, a notice revoking the offer was published. Shuey, unaware that the offer had been revoked, reported information on the whereabouts of Surratt to the proper U.S. government officials. The information furnished by Shuey led to Surratt's arrest. (Based on Shuey v. United States, 92 US 73, 23 L Ed 697, 1875)

1. Was Shuey legally entitled to the reward? Explain your answer.

____

____

____

____ 1.______

2. If Shuey had provided the information on Surratt before the reward offer had been revoked, would he be entitled to $25,000? Explain why or why not.

____

____

____

____ 2.______

Activity—Word Search

The 10 words listed below are important terms related to this chapter. The words read forward, backward, up, down, or diagonally, but always in a straight line and never skipping letters. Circle each word you find.

SCORE

R	S	S	M	N	L	X	K	T	E	X	S	Y
E	E	R	E	F	F	O	L	N	R	M	T	A
F	L	B	N	K	C	A	R	E	O	I	M	C
F	N	L	S	M	A	H	F	R	L	O	H	C
O	M	T	B	N	X	F	L	I	R	Q	U	E
R	G	B	D	F	O	M	B	I	D	R	P	P
E	O	N	B	A	F	I	G	K	O	M	S	T
T	H	O	O	N	S	Q	T	R	M	X	L	A
N	T	I	Y	S	P	B	E	C	N	A	O	N
U	H	T	O	L	S	F	B	M	E	M	E	C
O	L	P	X	B	F	V	A	N	S	J	L	E
C	M	O	N	O	I	T	A	C	O	V	E	R
I	B	K	L	C	V	I	C	O	P	T	I	R

offer
acceptance
offeror
offeree
bid
rejection
counteroffer
revocation
impossibility
option

UNIT 2 CONTRACTS

Chapter 8 Consideration

NAME______________________________ DATE__________

SCORE__________

Study Guide and Review

PART 1: For each statement, write the letter of the best answer in the Answers column. *ANSWERS* *SCORE*

1. An agreement is unenforceable because of lack of consideration when (A) consideration is inadequate, (B) consideration is not in the form of money, (C) a person gives up legal rights, (D) no promise is given or act completed for the offeror's promise. ______ 1.______
2. Lee owed Chaney $450. Both Lee and Chaney agreed on the amount owed. The debt would be discharged if (A) Chaney accepted $300 and a set of books worth $125 from Lee, (B) Chaney accepted $375 in full payment, (C) Chaney accepted $400 in full payment, (D) Chaney orally agreed to cancel the debt. ______ 2.______
3. After Buck found Conrad's wallet, Conrad orally promised to pay Buck $15. Conrad is not legally bound to pay because the consideration for her promise was (A) present, (B) past, (C) future, (D) illegal. ______ 3.______
4. Altier orally promised his daughter a silver bracelet as a gift. Altier is not legally bound because (A) a promise to make a gift is unenforceable, (B) he never intended to give this gift, (C) the consideration was inadequate, (D) the gift was too expensive. ______ 4.______
5. When a debtor and a creditor disagree on the amount owed on a debt and agree to compromise, the debt is (A) legally not paid, (B) legally not binding, (C) legally settled, (D) partially settled. ______ 5.______
6. A police officer is not entitled to a reward offered for the arrest of a criminal because (A) the officer has a legal duty to arrest criminals, (B) a reward is not legal consideration, (C) the reward is not an offer, (D) the reward is too high. ______ 6.______
7. Your uncle gave you a TV. He could not claim lack of consideration and demand its return because (A) a promise of a gift is unenforceable, (B) the TV is future consideration, (C) consideration is unimportant once an agreement is executed, (D) the consideration was inadequate. ______ 7.______
8. McIntyre was struck by a car driven by Gaines, who orally promised McIntyre $500 if she would not bring suit for the injuries. McIntyre agreed. McIntyre (A) has made a void agreement, (B) is entitled only to actual expenses, (C) has no rights because she gave no consideration for Gaines' promise, (D) has a right to $500 because she refrained from doing what she had a legal right to do. ______ 8.______
9. Conrad owed Scott $800, but was unable to pay Scott on the due date. Scott agreed to let Conrad pay him the following month. This agreement (A) is not legally binding, (B) is legally binding, (C) is enforceable by Conrad, (D) contains adequate consideration by Scott. ______ 9.______
10. Allen repaired Hansen's house while Hansen was ill. When she found out about the repairs, Hansen promised to pay Allen $50. Hansen's promise is not enforceable in a court of law because it was (A) not adequate, (B) for past consideration, (C) for future consideration, (D) too indefinite. ______ 10.______

PART 2: For each of the following case problems, give a decision by writing "yes" or "no." Then, in sentence form, give a reason for your decision.

SCORE

1. Adler was a medical research assistant at Mills General Hospital. Before his contract with the hospital expired, he was offered a position with another hospital at a higher salary. Mills General Hospital then offered Adler an increase in salary if he would complete his employment contract. Adler then promised to stay at Mills General Hospital. Is Adler entitled to the increase in salary offered by the hospital?

Decision: ______________________________

Reason: ______________________________

____

______________________________ 1. ______

2. Gurbowski, who was heavily in debt, offered to sell her cycle valued at $1,200 for $800 to Marconi. Marconi accepted the offer. After thinking about the offer, Gurbowski decided not to deliver the cycle, claiming that $800 was not enough. Is Marconi entitled to delivery of the cycle?

Decision: ______________________________

Reason: ______________________________

____

______________________________ 2. ______

3. Visca, who was visiting a friend's house, was injured by a ceiling tile that fell and hit her on the head. The friend gave her money for one visit to a doctor and for prescriptions ordered by the doctor. In return, Visca agreed not to sue for injuries. Later Visca complained of severe headaches and had to see a doctor several times and continue on medication. Visca then decided to sue for additional money. Can Visca collect?

Decision: ______________________________

Reason: ______________________________

____

____

______________________________ 3. ______

4. Mr. Springer promised to give his son James a car on his 20th birthday. Is Mr. Springer legally bound by this promise?

Decision: ______________________________

Reason: ______________________________

____

______________________________ 4. ______

UNIT 2 CONTRACTS

Chapter 9 Competent Parties

NAME ____________________ DATE ____________

SCORE ____________

Study Guide and Review

PART 1: For each statement, write the letter of the best answer in the Answers column. *ANSWERS* *SCORE*

1. Kavik has been declared legally insane by a court. Her purchase of an electric corn popper for $43.95 is (A) voidable by Kavik, (B) void, (C) valid if the price of the corn popper is reasonable, (D) valid if the store declares it valid. ________ 1.______
2. Two months before reaching the age of majority, Marci bought a radar detector for $129.95. She paid cash. Nine months later, she sought to avoid the agreement. Marci's delay in avoiding the agreement (A) made her liable to the merchant for fraud, (B) did not prevent her from avoiding the agreement, (C) most likely constituted a ratification of the agreement, (D) entitled her to only a partial refund of the purchase price. ________ 2.______
3. A minor who disaffirms an executed agreement with an adult (A) is bound for life, (B) ends the agreement with no further obligation, (C) must inform the adult orally, (D) must return any consideration received from the adult. ________ 3.______
4. An emancipated minor who purchases a prescription in a drug store is required to pay (A) any amount the druggist wants to charge, (B) the reasonable value of the prescription, (C) an amount decided upon by the minor, (D) the price set by the manufacturer. ________ 4.______
5. Lewis, a minor, sold her indoor exerciser to Francis, an adult. Francis then resold the exerciser to Beacon, a good faith purchaser. Beacon's title is (A) voidable, (B) valid, (C) void, (D) unenforceable. ________ 5.______
6. Agreements of persons who suffer from periods of temporary insanity but who have not been declared legally insane by a court may be disaffirmed by (A) the temporarily insane person upon becoming sane, (B) the temporarily insane person while either sane or temporarily insane, (C) the other party to the agreement, (D) either party. ________ 6.______
7. Cigarette lighters, jewelry, and electronic games are legally classified as (A) necessaries, (B) luxury items, (C) adult items, (D) entertainment items. ________ 7.______
8. Thompson, a minor, bought headphones for her stereo from The Stereo Store. This agreement is (A) voidable by The Stereo Store only, (B) voidable by either party, (C) voidable by Thompson only, (D) binding on both parties. ________ 8.______
9. An emancipated minor may avoid agreements to pay for (A) having a tooth filled by a dentist, (B) jeans and shirts that are part of a school wardrobe, (C) room and board at a private roominghouse, (D) archery equipment used in sports tournaments. ________ 9.______
10. An emancipated minor's contracts are voidable unless they are (A) for luxury items, (B) for necessaries, (C) made with other minors, (D) made with adults. ________ 10.______
11. A person who enters into a written contract while intoxicated and does not understand the consequences of the agreement (A) is still bound by the written contract, (B) may avoid the contract under certain conditions on becoming sober, (C) must live with the consequences of the act and can do nothing, (D) waives all rights in that agreement. ________ 11.______
12. The best illustration of a legally competent party is (A) a person under the influence of alcohol, (B) a 14-year-old, (C) a 65-year-old, (D) a legally insane person. ________ 12.______

PART 2: In each of the following case problems, give a decision by writing "yes" or "no." Then, in sentence form, give a reason for your decision.

SCORE

1. A month before his 18th birthday, Karlson purchased a VCR for $450 from Langley. He agreed in writing to pay $50 down and the balance in monthly payments of $40. After making 3 payments, Karlson tried to return the VCR and have his money refunded, less depreciation. Was he within his legal rights in returning the VCR and asking for a refund?

Decision: ______________________________

Reason: ______________________________

____

____

______________________________ 1. ______

2. Cordaro, age 17, who is self-supporting, injured herself while cycling across the country. The injury was serious enough to require immediate medical attention. After being treated by a physician, Cordaro refused to pay the bill, claiming that her parents were still liable for her medical bills. Is Cordaro's refusal legal?

Decision: ______________________________

Reason: ______________________________

______________________________ 2. ______

3. Roper, age 17½, bought a new car for her personal use. A few days after her 18th birthday, she asked the dealer to take the car back. Could Roper disaffirm this contract?

Decision: ______________________________

Reason: ______________________________

____

______________________________ 3. ______

4. Gruscho, owner of London Bridge Men's Store, sold a tuxedo to Robbins. Robbins, who was only 17, claimed to be 20. He agreed to pay the $250 purchase price in 30 days. After the 30 days passed, Robbins returned the tuxedo, which he had worn twice, and disaffirmed the purchase. Gruscho refused to accept the tuxedo. He sued Robbins, claiming that Robbins lied about his age and that a used tuxedo had no value. Can Gruscho legally refuse to take back the tuxedo and sue Robbins?

Decision: ______________________________

Reason: ______________________________

____

____

______________________________ 4. ______

UNIT 2 CONTRACTS

Chapter 10 Legal Purpose

NAME________________________ DATE__________

SCORE__________

Study Guide and Review

PART 1: For each of the following case problems, give a decision by writing "yes" or "no" in the space provided. Then, in sentence form, give a reason for your answer.

SCORE

1. In return for his daughter's promise never to marry, Wesson agreed to give her $25,000. Is this an enforceable agreement?

   Decision: ________________________

   Reason: ________________________

   ________________________ 1.______

2. Lane promised $5000 to an assemblyperson if he would influence the legislature to pass a certain law. Is this an enforceable agreement?

   Decision: ________________________

   Reason: ________________________

   ____

   ________________________ 2.______

3. Quinn agreed to pay Thorpe $500 if she would not testify against him in a court trial. Thorpe did not testify against Quinn. Is she entitled to the $500?

   Decision: ________________________

   Reason: ________________________

   ________________________ 3.______

4. Kulp, although not a properly licensed real estate agent, sold a house for Curtis. Can Kulp legally collect for his services?

   Decision: ________________________

   Reason: ________________________

   ____

   ________________________ 4.______

SCORE

5. Wenly sold her retail dress shop in Boston to Ryan, agreeing not to engage in a similar business within 5 blocks of the present location for one year. Is Wenly bound by such an agreement?

Decision: ______

Reason: ______

______ 5. ______

6. Beaton, owner of a grocery store, promised to supply Marvin, the mayor, with free food for the next year if an ordinance favorable to Beaton was passed by the city council. Is this agreement binding on Beaton?

Decision: ______

Reason: ______

______

______ 6. ______

7. Rissone received a letter from a magazine publisher inviting her to enter the company's $6,000,000 sweepstakes promotion by simply returning a book of certificates with her name already typed on them. In the same envelope was an invitation to buy one of the company's new books called *Eat Better, Live Better* at a reduced price. She did not have to buy the book in order to enter the sweepstakes, however. Rissone returned the certificates, but she did not win anything. She was so irritated that she called the company and told them that they were carrying on an illegal operation. Is Rissone correct?

Decision: ______

Reason: ______

______

______

______ 7. ______

PART 2: For each statement, write the letter of the best answer in the Answers column. ANSWERS SCORE

1. Usury laws provide protection in a contract (A) for the loan of money, (B) for the sale of merchandise on credit, (C) to be performed on Sunday, (D) for the restraint of trade. ______ 1. ______
2. A statute that requires a person to obtain a license to practice a certain trade or profession without having to show competence in that trade or profession is a (A) criminal statute, (B) usury statute, (C) prohibiting statute, (D) revenue-raising statute. ______ 2. ______
3. An example of a licensing statute is one that (A) requires an attorney to have a permit to practice law, (B) prevents usury, (C) restricts business activity on Sunday, (D) reasonably restricts trade. ______ 3. ______
4. Aaron bet Davis that a certain candidate would win the presidential election. Aaron's candidate won the election, but Davis refused to pay the bet. In most states, Aaron could not legally enforce the agreement because (A) a gambling agreement is illegal and void, (B) the agreement involves usury, (C) the bet was not in writing, (D) Aaron and Davis are both professional gamblers. ______ 4. ______

NAME____ DATE______________

ANSWERS SCORE

5. If an agreement is partially legal and partially illegal, (A) the entire agreement is void in all cases, (B) the legal part of the agreement may be enforced if it can be separated from the illegal part, (C) the legal part of the agreement is never enforceable, (D) the parties to the agreement may choose to enforce that part of the agreement that is beneficial to each one. ________ 5.______

6. If both parties know that an agreement is illegal, a court will probably (A) enforce the agreement, (B) refuse to hear the case, (C) allow the agreement to be ratified, (D) permit each party to recover any consideration given. ________ 6.______

7. Charging interest in excess of the legal rate is considered (A) restraint of trade, (B) enforceable, (C) usury, (D) *stare decisis*. ________ 7.______

8. An example of an agreement that would ordinarily be classified as illegal is one that (A) is entered into on a weekday after regular business hours, (B) is in reasonable restraint of trade, (C) involves usury, (D) is between an adult and a minor. ________ 8.______

9. A person whose main livelihood is gambling is classified as a (A) professional gambler, (B) semi-professional gambler, (C) casual gambler, (D) public gambler. ________ 9.______

10. An agreement that is in unreasonable restraint of trade is (A) enforceable, (B) void, (C) voidable, (D) valid. ________ 10.______

11. Billings and Durrick, competing distributors, made an agreement whereby Billings promised not to sell his goods in a specific area and Durrick promised not to sell his goods in another specified area. They made this agreement to keep prices high by eliminating competition. This arrangement is (A) legal because it reasonably restrains trade in order to control prices, (B) legal because a binding contract was made willingly by both parties, (C) illegal because it unreasonably restrains trade by controlling prices and territories, (D) illegal because agreements that allow manufacturers to set prices are void under the UCC. ________ 11.______

12. Maile agrees to sell his retail men's shop in Cleveland to Lunger. Lunger wants a clause restricting competition by Maile included in the contract. Which of these restrictive clauses would be enforceable: (A) never to engage in a similar business in Cleveland, (B) not to engage in a similar business in Ohio for the next 2 years, (C) not to engage in any type of business anywhere in Cleveland for the next year, (D) not to engage in a men's shop business within a radius of one mile for the next year. ________ 12.______

13. Which of the following actions is opposed to public policy: (A) an offer to pay money to a witness to testify falsely in court, (B) an offer to pay a contractor extra money to speed up a job he is already legally bound to do, (C) an offer to pay money to neighbors to attend your birthday party, (D) an offer to pay a lawyer to represent your civic group at a legislative session on a bill seeking tax reduction. ________ 13.______

14. Slater, believing that his daughter was about to marry and leave him, offered to pay her $10,000 if she would promise never to marry. The daughter promised and accepted the $10,000. One year later, she married. Slater sued for breach of contract. A court would probably rule that Slater is entitled to (A) recover nothing, (B) recover the $10,000, (C) recover the $10,000 plus interest, (D) annul the marriage on the basis of fraud. ________ 14.______

15. Which agreement would ordinarily be considered illegal: (A) an agreement between two people that one would pay the other $20 depending on the outcome of a football game, (B) a contract made by a married woman who is a minor, (C) a lobbying agreement, (D) none of these answers. ________ 15.______

16. An agreement to engage in a bank robbery is an example of a (A) quasi-contract, (B) voidable contract, (C) void contract, (D) contract implied in law. ________ 16.______

Activity—Case Analysis

Study the case described below and then answer the questions that follow. *SCORE*

The Crown Oak Novelty Company (plaintiff) sued the Fun and Games Entertainment Center (defendant) for breach of contract to recover the purchase price of checkers and checkerboards sold to the defendant. At the trial, the defendant's attorney stated that (a) the checkerboards were used as games of chance at the entertainment center, and (b) games of chance are prohibited by state law. The defendant's attorney further stated, "Since the plaintiff knew these facts, the contract with the entertainment center was illegal, void, and unenforceable. Therefore, my client does not have to pay for the merchandise."

The plaintiff's attorney admitted that Crown Oak knew the checkerboards were being used at the entertainment center, but argued that checkers is a game of skill, not chance. In a game of chance (throwing dice, for example), luck is the dominant feature; in a game of skill, ability and skill in playing the game are the dominant features. The plaintiff's attorney pointed out that only players with enough skill in playing checkers could solve the checker problems used at the Fun and Games Entertainment Center. He then introduced a copy of the relevant state law to show that only games of chance, not games of skill, were prohibited. The court ruled in favor of the plaintiff and ordered the defendant to pay for the checkerboards and checkers.

1. On what basis did Crown Oak Novelty sue the Fun and Games Entertainment Center?

____ 1. ______

2. On what basis did the Fun and Games Entertainment Center deny liability? ______________

____

____

____ 2. ______

3. Did the court agree with the Fun and Games Entertainment Center? ______________

____

____ 3. ______

4. What evidence was introduced to convince the court to decide the way it did? ______________

____

____ 4. ______

5. Assume that the defendant's argument is correct. What responsibility does the defendant have to pay the plaintiff as the result of this lawsuit?

____

____

____

____ 5. ______

UNIT 2 CONTRACTS

Chapter 11 Oral and Written Contracts

NAME________________________ DATE__________

SCORE__________

Study Guide and Review

PART 1: Indicate whether each statement below is true or false by circling either "true" or "false" in the Answers column.

	ANSWERS		*SCORE*
1. In a contract of guaranty, the guarantor's promise to pay is secondary to the debtor's promise.	true	false	1.______
2. Except as provided by statute, oral contracts are just as enforceable as written contracts.	true	false	2.______
3. The statute of frauds applies only to executory contracts.	true	false	3.______
4. One advantage of a written contract over an oral contract is that a written contract needs no witnesses to establish its existence and terms.	true	false	4.______
5. An oral promise to pay your own debt is not enforceable.	true	false	5.______
6. The parties to a written contract are usually bound by the terms in the agreement.	true	false	6.______
7. A court usually allows oral evidence to change the terms of a written agreement.	true	false	7.______
8. Martin agreed to work for Slim for 13 months. This agreement would be enforceable if made over the phone.	true	false	8.______
9. Parol evidence may be admitted in court to explain vague terms in a written contract.	true	false	9.______
10. A written contract may be changed by a subsequent oral agreement if the written contract was not required by the statute of frauds to be in writing.	true	false	10.______

PART 2: In each of the following case problems, give a decision by writing "yes" or "no." Then, in sentence form, give a reason for your decision.

SCORE

1. Marks tried to purchase some goods on credit from Bellows. Bellows refused to sell him the goods because he did not believe Marks would be able to pay. Minks orally promised Bellows that he would pay for the goods if Marks failed to do so. If Bellows sells the goods to Marks, is Minks legally bound by his promise?

   Decision: ____

   Reason: ____

   ____ 1.______

2. DeRoller was the executor of his mother's estate. Since there were insufficient funds in the estate to pay all its debts, DeRoller orally promised several creditors that he would pay the balance out of his own funds. Can DeRoller be held legally responsible for his promise?

   Decision: ____

   Reason: ____

   ____ 2.______

SCORE

3. Bain orally agreed to sell some land to Carroll for $10,000 and accepted a deposit of $1,000 to bind the agreement. Later, upon learning that another buyer would pay a higher price, Bain refused to honor the contract with Carroll. Carroll sued to enforce the contract. Will Carroll succeed in this suit?

Decision: ____________________

Reason: ____________________

____

____________________ 3. ______

4. On July 15, 1988, Martin orally agreed to work for Stein until June 1, 1989. Is this contract enforceable?

Decision: ____________________

Reason: ____________________

____________________ 4. ______

5. Moralle orally promised Hanson that if she agreed to marry him, he would give her a large monthly expense account, a new car every two years, and a vacation trip each year to a destination of her choice. Hanson accepted the promise, and they were married. Moralle, however, did not keep his promises. Hanson sued for damages. Will she succeed in this suit?

Decision: ____________________

Reason: ____________________

____________________ 5. ______

PART 3: For each statement, write the letter of the best answer in the Answers column. ANSWERS SCORE

1. Sol telephoned the Ace Pet Store and told the owner to deliver to his fiancee the French poodle he (Sol) had looked at the day before. Sol asked that the cost of the dog be charged to his account. The pet was delivered. This agreement is (A) binding on Sol because it is an oral promise to pay another's debt, (B) binding on Sol because it is an oral promise to pay his own debt, (C) not binding on Sol because an oral promise to pay another's debt is not binding, (D) not binding on Sol because there was no consideration for the oral promise. ______ 1. ______
2. Abbot accepted Milligan's oral offer to sell a small parcel of real property. This agreement is (A) illegal since it should have been in writing, (B) illegal because the sale was not arranged by a licensed real estate salesperson, (C) legal but unenforceable by either party, (D) legal but enforceable only by the offeror. ______ 2. ______
3. Yockel agreed to work for Schnabel for 18 months. This agreement would be enforceable if made (A) in a face-to-face conversation, (B) over the telephone, (C) through an exchange of telegrams, (D) orally through a friend. ______ 3. ______
4. Parol evidence is admissible to show that (A) terms had been added to the original contract, (B) the original contract had been changed, (C) one party was persuaded to make the contract by fraud on the part of the other party, (D) the contract does not show the real intentions of the parties. ______ 4. ______

NAME____ DATE______________

		ANSWERS	SCORE
5.	The type of contract that arises when one person promises to pay another's debt if that person does not pay is (A) a contract of suretyship, (B) a contract of guaranty, (C) a contract for services, (D) a contract under seal.	______	5.______
6.	Long offered to sell Vickers, a neighbor, a 25-foot wide strip of land between their two lots so that Vickers would have room to build a garage. Vickers accepted the offer. This agreement would be binding on Long if (A) Vickers paid $100 for an option to buy, (B) it was made in the presence of at least two witnesses, (C) it was made in writing, (D) Long promised orally that he would sell.	______	6.______
7.	An example of an agreement that is binding even if it is *not* in writing is (A) a contract to borrow an automobile, (B) a contract to sell real property, (C) a contract with marriage as a consideration, (D) a contract to pay the debts of another person.	______	7.______
8.	In most states, the written evidence of an agreement required by the statute of frauds is (A) parol evidence, (B) a guaranty, (C) an executor, (D) an informal memorandum.	______	8.______
9.	If two parties fully perform an oral contract that should have been in writing, (A) either party can have the contract set aside because it was not in writing, (B) the statute of frauds no longer applies, (C) the contract is illegal, (D) the parties are guilty of fraud.	______	9.______
10.	If a contract is required to be in writing under the statute of frauds, modifications to that contract (A) are not binding, (B) can be made orally, (C) must be in writing, (D) require additional consideration.	______	10.______

Activity 1—Word Search

Find the words listed below relating to the chapter you have read. The words read forward, backward, up, down, and diagonally, but always in a straight line and never skipping letters. Circle each word you find.

SCORE

R	N	I	G	S	B	O	H	Q	U	A	T	X	Q	Y	Z
V	S	D	U	A	R	F	F	O	E	T	U	T	A	T	S
R	O	T	A	R	T	S	I	N	I	M	D	A	Z	R	M
O	P	A	R	O	L	E	V	I	D	E	N	C	E	E	U
L	E	C	A	S	F	L	N	G	N	C	G	T	X	P	D
Z	C	O	N	T	R	A	C	T	S	J	S	V	E	O	N
K	T	K	T	N	E	Y	I	C	E	K	R	P	C	R	A
O	D	E	Y	E	V	I	S	B	Q	F	N	C	U	P	R
W	N	S	I	S	C	E	K	U	H	W	B	J	T	L	O
A	I	J	A	A	F	G	H	S	T	K	O	P	O	A	M
L	D	C	V	E	O	S	Z	T	E	M	U	L	R	E	E
A	O	R	A	L	C	O	N	T	R	A	C	T	S	R	M

administrator
contracts
executor
guaranty
lease
memorandum
oral contracts
parol evidence
real property
statute of frauds

______

Activity 2—Writing a Contract

You have worked the past three summers and have saved $2,000. You now want to buy a used car. In the space below, write your own contract to buy the car. You are buying the car from an owner rather than a used-car dealer. Be sure to include all the elements of a valid contract in the contract you write.

UNIT 2 CONTRACTS

Chapter 12 The Termination of Contracts

NAME________________________________ DATE____________

SCORE____________

Study Guide and Review

PART 1: For each statement, write the letter of the best answer in the Answers column. *ANSWERS* *SCORE*

1. The voluntary surrender of a person's contractual rights is known as a (A) satisfaction, (B) tender, (C) novation, (D) waiver. ________ 1.______
2. When Johnson finished painting Bristol's house as agreed, Bristol paid him in full. Their contract was discharged by (A) accord and satisfaction, (B) tender, (C) performance, (D) operation of law. ________ 2.______
3. Kemp agreed to build a storage shed at the back of Martin's property. Before work began, the city passed an ordinance forbidding the construction of this and similar buildings in that neighborhood. As a result of this ordinance, (A) the contract was discharged, (B) Kemp was liable to Martin for breach, (C) the city was liable to Martin for damages, (D) the existing contract was not affected. ________ 3.______
4. An offer to fulfill the terms of a contract by completing an act required by the contract or by paying money is known as (A) novation, (B) ratification, (C) mutual agreement, (D) tender of performance. ________ 4.______
5. Vinton was under written contract to work for Rossi. Vinton had to move to another state and received from Rossi a written release from his original agreement. This contract was discharged by (A) performance, (B) mutual agreement, (C) breach, (D) subsequent impossibility. ________ 5.______
6. Nash, a rock celebrity, was under contract to give a concert in the Warner Theater. Serious illness prevented her from giving the concert on the agreed date. In this situation, (A) Nash is released from the contract and is not liable for any damages or losses incurred by the Warner Theater, (B) Nash is released from the contract but is liable for damages or losses incurred by the theater, (C) Nash has the right to give the concert when she recovers from her illness, (D) the Warner Theater is obligated to accept performance by another celebrity whom Nash sends as her substitute. ________ 6.______
7. Gibbons entered into a written agreement with Bensinger to purchase a painting. In the meantime, without the knowledge of either party, the painting was destroyed in a fire. This contract was discharged by (A) performance, (B) breach, (C) mutual agreement, (D) impossibility. ________ 7.______
8. The refusal of a tender of payment (A) forces a settlement by arbitration, (B) forces payment with legal tender, (C) does not excuse the debtor from paying interest charges, (D) does not discharge the obligation. ________ 8.______
9. The usual manner of discharging a contract is by (A) subsequent impossibility, (B) death of one of the parties, (C) assignment, (D) performance. ________ 9.______
10. When Rosco was unable to pay the $1,000 he owed Lyden, Lyden agreed to let Rosco paint Lyden's house in payment. When Rosco finished painting the house, his original obligation was discharged by (A) breach, (B) impossibility of performance, (C) accord and satisfaction, (D) disability. ________ 10.______
11. A change made in the terms of an executory contract by one party without the knowledge and consent of the other party is called (A) a novation, (B) a substitution, (C) an accord, (D) an alteration. ________ 11.______

12. Vasquez contracted to install vinyl siding on O'Grady's house during the first two weeks of August. When Vasquez arrived on August 1 to begin the work, O'Grady told him that the job would have to be postponed for two months. Vasquez's obligation to perform the contract was discharged by (A) tender of performance, (B) operation of law, (C) agreement, (D) delegation of duty.

ANSWERS	SCORE
________	12. ______

PART 2: Read the following news story and then answer the question in the space provided. SCORE

COURT PENALIZES ROCK SINGER FOR NOT SINGING

ROCHESTER, N.Y. (AP)—A state supreme court judge placed a $25,000 judgment on Mike Zoe, well-known rock star, for failing to perform in concert at the Community War Memorial Auditorium on three successive nights. The Honorable Richard Bloom ruled yesterday in favor of the owners of the Community War Memorial Auditorium, who complained that Zoe ignored a contractual agreement to perform three concerts.

1. Under what circumstances could Zoe be excused from paying damages for not appearing?

____

____

____

____ 1. ______

PART 3: In the Answers column at the right, write the word "true" if the statement is true. If the underlined word or phrase makes the statement false, substitute the word or phrase needed to make the statement true.

	ANSWERS	SCORE
1. If one party to a contract makes a material change in its terms without the other party's permission, the contract is discharged by <u>novation</u>.	________	1. ______
2. A contract is discharged by <u>full performance</u> when a person in good faith fulfills all the major requirements leaving only minor details incomplete.	________	2. ______
3. <u>Full performance</u> is the most common method by which contracts are discharged.	________	3. ______
4. The offer to perform the terms of a contract or to pay money is called <u>substantial performance</u>.	________	4. ______
5. If the subject matter that is essential to the performance of the contract is destroyed through no fault of either party, the contract is considered to be <u>discharged</u>.	________	5. ______
6. To <u>waive</u> is to mutually agree to cancel a contract even after one or both parties have completely performed.	________	6. ______
7. If a new agreement is made before the original contract is breached, this new agreement is called a <u>substitute contract</u>.	________	7. ______
8. When Wes finished repairing Thomas's car as agreed, Thomas paid Wes in full. The contract was discharged by <u>operation of law</u>.	________	8. ______
9. Lund and Mann entered into a contract. Two months later, they agreed to let Wells perform Mann's obligations with Lund releasing Mann from her agreement. In this case, Mann's obligations are discharged by <u>accord and satisfaction</u>.	________	9. ______
10. The form of money accepted as lawful payment of debts in the United States is called <u>legal tender</u>.	________	10. ______

NAME ______________________________ DATE ____________

Activity—Learning How Contracts End

Read the following contract and then answer the questions on page 46.

PROPERTY LEASE

I, Harriet M. Cole, of 242 Marion Street, Denver, Colorado, agree to lease the premises of 1254 Stillmeadow Drive, Denver, Colorado, to Janet L. and William T. Percy, for a period of two (2) years, beginning March 1, 19--. The tenants are to pay rent of six hundred and fifty dollars ($650.00) per month, with rent being due on the first (1st) day of each month. The premises are to be used as a residence for Janet L. and William T. Percy and are not to be used for any other purposes. Tenants may not sublease premises without the express, written permission of Harriet M. Cole. At the end of this lease, tenants will give up possession of these premises in as good condition as they now are, excepting normal wear, accidents, fire, and other acts of God.

If tenants fail to pay rent when due or fail to vacate the premises upon expiration of this lease, it is agreed that tenants will pay double the rent specified above for the time the rent remains due and unpaid or the time the tenant fails to give possession.

Signed this third (3rd) day of February, 19--.

Harriet M. Cole
Harriet M. Cole

Janet L. Percy
Janet L. Percy

William T. Percy
William T. Percy

SCORE

1. Does this contract meet the requirements of a valid contract? Explain how this contract does or does not meet these requirements.

1. ______

2. In what ways may this contract be terminated?

2. ______

3. What conditions must occur for this contract to be performed in full?

3. ______

4. How might this contract be discharged by impossibility?

4. ______

5. How might this contract terminate by breach of contract?

5. ______

6. If the tenants breach this contract, are damages provided for in the contract? If so, what are the damages?

6. ______

UNIT 2 CONTRACTS

Chapter 13 Breach of Contract

NAME____________________ DATE__________

SCORE__________

Study Guide and Review

PART 1: For each statement, write the letter of the best answer in the Answers column.

	ANSWERS	*SCORE*
1. In seeking damages, the victim of a breach of contract has a duty to (A) increase the amount of the damages, (B) mitigate damages, (C) liquidate the damages, (D) rescind the contract.	______	1.______
2. Aman had a written employment contract with Bagden for one year at a $48,000 salary, payable at the rate of $4,000 a month. Aman worked for five months, collected $20,000, and then was discharged without cause. Within a few days, he found another job at a lower salary and sued Bagden for breach of contract. The greatest amount that Aman may legally recover is (A) $48,000, (B) $28,000, (C) $28,000 minus his earnings on the new job, (D) $20,000 minus his earnings on the new job.	______	2.______
3. Marriott agreed to do some electrical work for Bastiuk for $500. The terms of the contract called for one half of the contract price to be paid once the work began. When Marriott began work and requested $250, Bastiuk offered only $175. Bastiuk's action would be considered (A) substantial performance, (B) alteration, (C) breach of contract, (D) rescission.	______	3.______
4. Manix sued Cartright for breach of contract. The court awarded Manix damages of $1. This award is known as (A) liquidated damages, (B) nominal damages, (C) premeditated damages, (D) mitigated damages.	______	4.______
5. Falvo entered into a contract with Mathis to build an addition to Mathis's house. The price agreed upon was $25,000. Falvo failed to do the work, so Mathis contracted with Baily to do the work for $24,000. Mathis then sued Falvo for breach of contract and sought $1,000 in damages. The court will likely rule (A) in Mathis's favor for $1,000, because Falvo breached the contract, (B) in Mathis's favor, but for nominal damages only, (C) in Falvo's favor because Mathis did not suffer a loss, (D) in Falvo's favor because Mathis saved money as a result of the breach.	______	5.______
6. The statute of limitations (A) specifies the time within which a lawsuit may be started, (B) requires that certain contracts be in writing, (C) requires the use of written evidence of an action at a trial, (D) contains the same provisions in all states of the United States.	______	6.______
7. Feingold contracted to sell to Betz for $25,000 an original letter written by George Washington. Both thought the letter was authentic. However, the letter turned out to be a reproduction. Betz now wishes to avoid the contract. The most appropriate remedy is (A) punitive damages, (B) compensatory damages, (C) specific performance, (D) rescission of the contract.	______	7.______
8. The basis of fraud is (A) a misrepresentation of opinion, (B) an act of violence, (C) a threat of force, (D) concealment or misrepresentation of a material fact.	______	8.______
9. Perry sold an old ring to Weeks for $10. Later Perry learned that the ring was worth $500. If Perry sues, she is legally entitled to recover (A) $500, (B) the ring, (C) $490, (D) nothing.	______	9.______
10. Which of the following is *not* a legal reason for exercising the right to rescind a contract: (A) duress, (B) minority, (C) unilateral mistake, (D) fraud.	______	10.______

PART 2: Indicate whether each statement below is true or false by circling either "true" or "false" in the Answers column.

	ANSWERS		SCORE
1. One of the elements necessary to establish fraud is a false statement or concealment of a material fact.	true	false	1. ______
2. Money damages awarded to an injured party should by law place this person in the same position he or she would have been in if the contract had been carried out.	true	false	2. ______
3. Undue influence renders a contract voidable by either party.	true	false	3. ______
4. A mutual mistake about the identity of the subject matter does not affect the validity of the contract.	true	false	4. ______
5. Gugel, a used-car dealer, told Billings, a prospective customer, "This is the best used-car value in town." Relying on this statement, Gugel bought the car, but soon discovered that the car had been substantially overpriced. Billings may avoid this contract on the basis of fraud.	true	false	5. ______
6. When money damages do not adequately and fairly compensate for a loss, the injured party can sue for specific performance or request a court to issue an injunction.	true	false	6. ______
7. Neilson requested a catalog from Noom Brothers. She used an order form to order some jewelry, but entered an incorrect catalog number. As a result, she received jewelry she did not want. Neilson has a legal right to return the jewelry because her mistake voided the contract.	true	false	7. ______
8. Specific performance is generally granted in contracts for the sale of real property.	true	false	8. ______
9. A person who conceals a material fact is guilty of fraud if the concealment prevents the victim from discovering the truth.	true	false	9. ______
10. A court will not enforce a liquidated damages clause if the stated amount appears to be a penalty.	true	false	10. ______

Activity 1—Word Puzzle

Complete the following puzzle using the clues given below the puzzle. When you finish the puzzle, you will have a rule of law.

SCORE

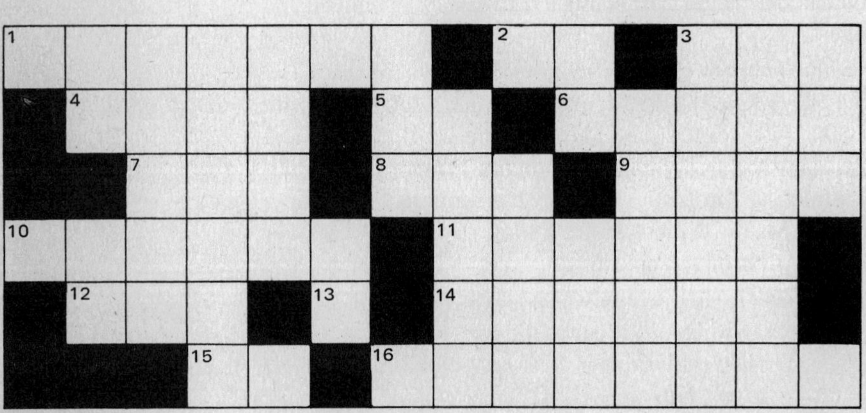

______

Clues:

1. Awarded to a person who is harmed by a breach of contract.
2. A common preposition.
3. A common article.
4. A word meaning "to have structure."
5. A common preposition.
6. Legal tender.
7. A common verb.
8. A common article.
9. A word meaning "the greatest in number."
10. A word meaning "widespread or generally known."
11. A word meaning "to correct a wrong or to enforce a legal right."
12. A common preposition.
13. A common article.
14. A word meaning "a violation of a legal obligation."
15. A common preposition.
16. A legal agreement.

NAME ______________________________ DATE ______________

Activity 2—Analyzing a Contract

Read the contract shown below and then answer the questions on page 50.

PROPERTY STORAGE AGREEMENT

This agreement is made on June 9, 19--, between Robert S. Greeley of 149 East Rossmoyne Street, Troy, Ohio, and Manuel E. Leon of 1910 Harrision Avenue, Troy, Ohio.

Manuel Leon agrees to store the following goods in his warehouse at 310 McGrath Road, Troy, Ohio:

Mahogany dining room furniture consisting of one (1) oval dining table and eight (8) matching chairs
One (1) three-cushion sofa
Two (2) reclining lounge chairs
One (1) 9' x 12' yellow wool carpet
Two (2) three-drawer, walnut chests
One (1) rotating electric fan
One (1) glass and walnut table
Two (2) brass and ceramic table lamps with shades

It is agreed that the above property is currently undamaged and is to be returned upon termination of this contract in the same condition as it currently exists, excepting accidents, fire, and other acts of God.

Robert Greeley agrees to pay Manuel Leon the sum of fifty dollars ($50.00) per month to store this property. Payment is to begin July 1, 19--, and end June 1, 19--. Payment is due on the first day of each month. Upon termination of this contract, Robert Greeley will assume responsibility of having the furniture listed above removed from the warehouse at 310 McGrath Road.

If Robert Greeley fails to make payments as agreed, Manuel Leon has the right to sell, after notifying Robert Greeley of his intent, part or all of the stored property to satisfy any amounts due on this contract.

Robert Greeley
____
Robert Greeley

Manuel Leon
____
Manuel Leon

SCORE

1. When injury is caused by a breach of contract, what are the remedies generally available to the injured party?

1. ______

2. If Greeley breaches his duties under the contract on the preceding page, what specific remedies does Leon have?

2. ______

3. Would damages for a breach of contract by Greeley be compensatory, liquidated, or nominal? Explain your answer.

3. ______

4. Could Leon collect money damages from Greeley other than those provided for in the contract? Why or why not?

4. ______

5. If Greeley breaches this contract by failing to make the last three payments of $50 per month, and Leon sells some of the furniture for $250, how much money does Leon get? If there is any money left after payment of the amount owed to Leon, who gets this remaining money? Why?

5. ______

UNIT 2 CONTRACTS

Chapter 14 Assignment of Contract Rights

NAME________________________ DATE__________

SCORE__________

Study Guide and Review

PART 1: Read the following notification of assignment and then answer the questions that follow. Place your answers in the Answers column.

ANSWERS *SCORE*

DATE: September 25, 19—
TO: Jane Lu, 189 Factor Road, Cleveland, OH 44112
FROM: Brendon Associates, 1334 Duncan Avenue, Cleveland, OH 44112

We have purchased from Hyland Fence Company of Cleveland, Ohio, their entire interest in the account they have against you in the amount of one thousand five hundred fifty dollars ($1,550). Any payments or communications in regard to this account should be made to us.

1. According to this notification of assignment, what right is being assigned? (A) right to receive payment of money, (B) right to the delivery of goods, (C) right to personal services, (D) right to a personal skill. ________ 1.______
2. Brendon Associates is legally known as the (A) offeror, (B) assignor, (C) assignee, (D) promisee. ________ 2.______
3. The Hyland Fence Company is known as the (A) assignee, (B) offeror, (C) promisee, (D) assignor. ________ 3.______
4. Jane Lu is the (A) obligor, (B) obligee, (C) assignor, (D) creditor. ________ 4.______
5. Before receiving the notification, Lu informed the Hyland Fence Company that fencing worth $500 was damaged and was being returned. If Lu returns the merchandise, she will be liable to Brendon Associates for payment of (A) $1,550, (B) $1,050, (C) $1,000, (D) nothing. ________ 5.______

PART 2: Indicate whether each statement below is true or false by circling either "true" or "false" in the Answers column.

ANSWERS *SCORE*

1. An obligor is a party to a contract who transfers rights and obligations to other people through assignment. true false 1.______
2. Contract obligations that require a special skill or knowledge may not be transferred without permission. true false 2.______
3. There is no time limit on notifying an obligor of an assignment. true false 3.______
4. A notice of assignment must always be in writing. true false 4.______
5. Personal services contracts cannot be assigned without the permission of the person providing the service. true false 5.______
6. State statutes sometimes place restrictions on assignment of rights. true false 6.______
7. Past performance of a contract before receiving notice of an assignment does not reduce the obligor's responsibility to the assignee. true false 7.______
8. Contract rights may legally be transferred by an assignment. true false 8.______
9. Two rights that may be assigned without permission are the payment of money and the delivery of goods. true false 9.______
10. Assigning rights under a contract does not entitle the assignee to the same rights that the assignor had before the assignment. true false 10.______

PART 3: For each statement, write the letter of the best answer in the Answers column. *ANSWERS* *SCORE*

1. Rene owed Currie \$550. Currie transferred the contract to Butts. Which step should Butts take in order to make sure Rene pays her instead of Currie? (A) notify Rene of the transfer, (B) file the contract in the county clerk's office, (C) have the transfer drawn up by an attorney, (D) have Rene's signature witnessed by a notary public. ________ 1.______
2. When rights under a contract are assigned, the assignee receives the same rights as the (A) obligor, (B) debtor, (C) assignor, (D) executor. ________ 2.______
3. Renault entered into a contract with Craft to have some plumbing work done. Craft later delegated the work to Marsden, another licensed plumber. Which of the following statements is true: (A) Craft cannot legally delegate her contract obligations, (B) Craft is still responsible for making sure the obligation is carried out, (C) Craft can no longer be held liable if the contract is breached, (D) the contract is automatically terminated. ________ 3.______
4. Which statement concerning the assignment of contracts is *false:* (A) rights to the payment of money and to the delivery of goods may be assigned without consent, (B) some rights may be assigned automatically by law, (C) responsibilities to perform skilled work may be assigned without approval of all parties, (D) the party who delegates a responsibility remains liable for proper performance. ________ 4.______
5. Dr. Senour, a successful ophthalmologist, notified her patients that she had sold her practice to Dr. Horner, an equally competent ophthalmologist, and that Dr. Horner would now be responsible for their treatment. Which statement best describes this transaction's legal effect on the patients? (A) they could legally refuse to accept Dr. Horner's services, (B) they are legally bound to accept Dr. Horner's services, (C) they may legally accept the services of another ophthalmologist but only with Dr. Senour's consent, (D) they could sue Dr. Senour for malpractice. ________ 5.______

PART 4: For each of the following case problems, give a decision by writing "yes" or "no" in the space provided. Then, in sentence form, give a reason for your decision. *SCORE*

1. On May 2, Blacke's Hardware paid \$200 of the \$1,000 owed to Greene's Wholesalers for a previous purchase of lawn mowers. On May 15, Greene's transferred all customer accounts to the We Get Results Finance Company. Two weeks later, Blacke's Hardware paid Greene's an additional \$200 on account. Blacke's did not receive notice of the assignment until June 9. After receiving this notice, is Blacke's Hardware obligated to pay the We Get Results Finance Company anything more?

Decision: ____

Reason: ____

____

____

____

____

____

____

____

____ 1.______

NAME ______________________________ DATE ______________

2. Corey was hired as a pharmacist by the Daw Drug Company under a one-year contract. After six months, Daw's sold out to the Freese Drug Company and assigned Corey's contract to Freese. Is Corey obligated to work for Freese for the remainder of the contract period?

SCORE

Decision: ______________________________

Reason: ______________________________

____

____

______________________________ 2. ______

3. Dr. Christen, a well-known physician and cancer expert, was under contract to deliver a major address to a physicians' group in Washington, D.C. A month before the scheduled address, Dr. Christen had a heart attack and had to cancel his engagements for at least six months. He notified the physicians' group that he was sending his assistant, also a doctor, who had been working with him. Does the group have to accept the substitute?

Decision: ______________________________

Reason: ______________________________

____

____

______________________________ 3. ______

4. Cooke sold all the assets of her business, including the accounts receivable, to Nugent. Did Cooke have the right to assign her accounts receivable to Nugent?

Decision: ______________________________

Reason: ______________________________

____

______________________________ 4. ______

5. Victor hired Carbone, a mason, to build a patio in his backyard. Because Carbone took on too many other jobs, he engaged another mason to build the patio for Victor. Can Carbone legally delegate his duty under an existing contract?

Decision: ______________________________

Reason: ______________________________

____

______________________________ 5. ______

6. You arranged to take guitar lessons from a prominent local guitarist. You chose this guitar teacher because you wanted to study his unique playing style. When you arrived for your first lesson, you found that the guitarist's brother would be giving you lessons instead. Can you refuse to accept this arrangement?

SCORE

Decision: ______________________________

Reason: ______________________________

____

____

______________________________ 6. ______

7. Your landlord assigned to a third party his rent claim from you of $300. Since you were not notified of the assignment, you paid the landlord the $300. Your landlord then left town. Can the third party demand payment of the $300 from you?

Decision: ______________________________

Reason: ______________________________

____

______________________________ 7. ______

Activity—Word Search

The 10 words listed below are important terms related to assignment of contract rights. The words read forward, backward, up, down, or diagonally, but always in a straight line and never skipping letters. Circle each word you find.

SCORE

S	N	O	I	T	A	G	I	L	B	O	T
N	O	N	P	E	R	S	O	N	A	L	M
A	T	R	A	N	S	F	E	R	A	B	N
S	B	N	F	H	J	N	K	N	G	P	O
S	Q	A	E	T	U	W	O	X	S	B	I
I	Y	S	B	M	P	S	V	T	L	Y	T
G	F	S	N	C	N	D	H	I	I	C	A
N	H	I	J	E	L	G	G	U	V	C	G
E	K	G	P	X	I	O	I	D	L	K	E
E	L	N	M	R	R	B	L	S	D	N	L
Q	O	O	G	M	P	Q	R	H	S	I	E
N	Q	R	S	D	L	B	X	R	T	A	D

assignee
assignment
assignor
delegation
nonpersonal
notice
obligations
obligor
rights
transfer

______

UNIT 2 CONTRACTS

Review

NAME________________________ DATE__________

SCORE__________

Review

PART 1: Indicate whether each statement below is true or false by circling either "true" or "false" in the Answers column.

	ANSWERS		*SCORE*
1. In a contract, the value of the consideration given need not be equal in value to the consideration received.	true	false	1.______
2. One who has a right to receive money from another may transfer this right to a third person through the process of delegation.	true	false	2.______
3. According to the statute of limitations, certain debts are outlawed and the right to legal action is lost if the claim is not filed within a specific period of time.	true	false	3.______
4. A contract to answer for the obligations of others must be in writing.	true	false	4.______
5. If a debtor makes a voluntary partial payment after the due date, the time limit under the statute of limitations starts over from the date of payment.	true	false	5.______
6. Cilino said to Regal, "I'll sell you my video game system for $175 cash today." Regal replied, "I'll take it by paying you $100 today and the other $75 in 30 days." Regal's reply resulted in an accord and satisfaction.	true	false	6.______
7. Nonpersonal rights cannot be transferred without the other party's permission.	true	false	7.______
8. When money damages do not adequately compensate for a loss, one remedy is for the injured party to sue for specific performance.	true	false	8.______
9. Not all contracts must be in writing to be valid.	true	false	9.______
10. A minor's obligation to pay for necessaries is an express contract.	true	false	10.______

PART 2: For each statement, write the letter of the best answer in the Answers column.

	ANSWERS	*SCORE*
1. A contract that is completely enforceable against all parties unless and until a party legally entitled to avoid the contract does so is (A) valid, (B) void, (C) voidable, (D) performed.	________	1.______
2. On July 8, Varden wrote to Monty offering to sell Monty her used car for $525. The letter stated, "Offer subject to actual receipt of your acceptance no later than July 23." Monty mailed a letter of acceptance on July 21, which reached Varden on July 24. A valid contract was made (A) July 21, (B) July 23, (C) July 24, (D) never.	________	2.______
3. An agreement induced by fraud is (A) valid, (B) void, (C) voidable by the injured party, (D) voidable by either party.	________	3.______
4. Carter offered to sell Milford a used power lawnmower. Milford accepted the offer. This offer and acceptance is called (A) mutual assent, (B) compromise, (C) ratification, (D) payment of an option.	________	4.______
5. Paul borrowed $100 from Best and promised in writing to pay the debt on March 1. On the due date, Paul could not pay the full amount but offered Best $50 in cash and a watch worth $25. Best accepted. Was the debt discharged? (A) Yes. When a claim is disputed, a compromise figure is binding. (B) Yes. A debt is canceled if the creditor accepts as full payment a part payment in money plus additional property. (C) No. The consideration was inadequate. (D) No. The additional consideration is illegal.	________	5.______

	ANSWERS	SCORE
6. A contract must be in writing to be enforceable if it involves (A) payment of an excessive interest rate, (B) sale of goods worth $350, (C) sale of real property, (D) restraint of marriage.	______	6. ______
7. Contracts involving personal services may be assigned or delegated (A) under any conditions, (B) with consent of all parties involved, (C) under no circumstances, (D) with consent of only one of the parties.	______	7. ______
8. If a party proves that a contract has been breached but shows damages of only a few dollars, the injured party may be awarded (A) liquidated damages, (B) remote damages, (C) nominal damages, (D) punitive damages.	______	8. ______
9. In a personal services contract, if the person to perform the services dies, the contract is (A) terminated, (B) assigned to a relative, (C) considered breached, (D) ratified.	______	9. ______
10. Agreements in unreasonable restraint of trade are (A) voidable, (B) quasi-contracts, (C) illegal, (D) valid.	______	10. ______
11. An agreement in which the offeree gives something of value to the offeror to keep an offer open is called (A) a tender of performance, (B) a compromise agreement, (C) an option contract, (D) a promise.	______	11. ______
12. A minor may disaffirm a contract for the purchase of a stereo (A) during minority or within a reasonable time after reaching majority, (B) only during minority, (C) within one year from the date of the agreement, (D) only after reaching majority.	______	12. ______
13. An agreement that would be illegal and therefore void is (A) a contract in reasonable restraint of trade, (B) a contract to pay a usurious rate of interest, (C) a contract to extend the time of payment of a debt, (D) a contract to hold an offer open for a certain time.	______	13. ______
14. The purpose of awarding an injured party money damages for breach of contract is to (A) permit the injured party to avoid the contract, (B) punish the party that breached the contract, (C) compensate the injured party for the loss suffered, (D) permit the injured party to make a profit.	______	14. ______
15. Carlo had a written contract with Sanders to purchase some cattle. Unknown to either party, the cattle had died. The contract was discharged by (A) breach, (B) performance, (C) impossibility, (D) mutual agreement.	______	15. ______
16. The statute of frauds applies only to (A) executed contracts, (B) executory contracts, (C) quasi-contracts, (D) illegal contracts.	______	16. ______

PART 3: Indicate by a checkmark in the Answers column whether each agreement described below is valid, void, or voidable on the part of the party underlined in each sentence.

	Valid	Void	Voidable	SCORE
1. A minor contracted to purchase a motorcycle for his personal use.	______	______	______	1. ______
2. An adult contracted to purchase a VCR from a minor.	______	______	______	2. ______
3. An adult sold real estate without a license to do so.	______	______	______	3. ______
4. An adult thought by some people to be mentally ill makes a reasonable contract to purchase a necessity.	______	______	______	4. ______
5. A minor ratified an executory contract when he reached majority.	______	______	______	5. ______

Activity—Analyzing a Contract

Study the contract shown on pages 57–58. Decide whether this contract meets all the requirements for a valid contract and then answer the questions on page 58.

NAME______________________________ DATE____________

BILL OF SALE

That Sandra G. Lockwood, a single person,

of Marion *County, in the State of* Indiana *, ha* s *this day bargained and sold, and does hereby bargain, sell, assign, transfer, set over, and deliver to* S. Kathryn Long, a single person,

in Marion *County, in the State of* Indiana *, for the sum of* One Thousand ($1,000.00)-- *Dollars,*

to Sandra G. Lockwood *in hand paid, the receipt whereof is hereby acknowledged, the following described Chattels, Goods, and Personal Property in* Marion *County, State of* Indiana *, to-wit:*

One (1) living room suite, consisting of a sofa and two (2) chairs, one (1) Perricle refrigerator, and one (1) Western range.

In Witness Whereof, *The said* Sandra G. Lockwood

ha s *hereunto set* her *hand and seal this* 5th *day of* June *19* _ _

Signed, sealed, and delivered in presence of Sandra G. Lockwood .... *(Seal)*

Sandra G. Lockwood

Diane L. Durkee .... *(Seal)*

Benjamin Elkins .... *(Seal)*

STATE OF INDIANA, Marion County, ss:

Sandra G. Lockwood being duly sworn, on oath says she is

the grantor .... in the within bill of sale; that she is *the owner of every article of personal property herein described, and in possession of same, and that the same is free of all incumbrances and liens of every kind. And in this affiant makes oath for the purpose of inducing the sale herein stipulated.*

Sandra G. Lockwood (Seal)

Subscribed and sworn to before me, this 5th *day of* June, 19--.

Andrea Meehan *Notary Public*

My Commission Expires August, 19--

SCORE

1. Has the requirement of offer and acceptance been met for this contract? Explain your answer.

____

____

_______________ 1. ______

2. What is the consideration for this agreement? _______________

_______________ 2. ______

3. Is the consideration adequate? _______________ 3. ______

4. What effect does the adequacy or inadequacy of the consideration have on the agreement? Explain your answer.

____

_______________ 4. ______

5. Who are the parties to this agreement? _______________

_______________ 5. ______

6. Assuming that the parties to this agreement were of legal ages, does this agreement meet the requirement of competent parties?

____

_______________ 6. ______

7. Does this agreement meet the requirement of legal purpose? Why or why not?

____

_______________ 7. ______

UNIT 3 Purchase and Sale of Goods

Chapter 15 The Sales Contract

NAME________________________________ DATE____________

SCORE____________

Study Guide and Review

PART 1: Indicate whether each statement below is true or false by circling either "true" or "false" in the Answers column.

	ANSWERS		SCORE
1. Under the UCC, an agreement modifying a contract for the sale of goods needs no consideration to be binding.	true	false	1.______
2. A contract for the sale of goods costing under $500 may be oral or written.	true	false	2.______
3. If goods are sent COD, the buyer must first pay for these goods before inspecting them to determine whether they conform to the contract.	true	false	3.______
4. If goods conform to the contract and have been delivered properly, the buyer must accept and pay for these goods according to the contract terms.	true	false	4.______
5. The term "goods" includes intangible personal property such as shares of stock.	true	false	5.______
6. An oral contract for the sale of goods costing $500 or more is enforceable if the buyer makes full payment.	true	false	6.______
7. Under the UCC, it is important to determine whether buyers and sellers are merchants or nonmerchants.	true	false	7.______
8. An action for breach of a sales contract must be started within four years after the breach.	true	false	8.______
9. Mindy, a furniture dealer, sold her car to Martin. In this transaction, Mindy is considered to be a merchant according to the UCC.	true	false	9.______
10. Gibbons bought a record from his friend Mark. Mark is considered a merchant.	true	false	10.______

PART 2: For each statement, write the letter of the best answer in the Answers column.

	ANSWERS	SCORE
1. Under the UCC, after the buyer has been notified that the goods are ready for delivery, the proper place for delivery is (A) the seller's place of business, (B) the buyer's place of business, (C) a place designated by the buyer, (D) a point halfway between the seller's and the buyer's places of business.	________	1.______
2. Cuomo, owner of a large men's retail store, signed a written contract to purchase 100 dozen ties at $60 a dozen from the Gem Wholesale Company. The ties were shipped, and Cuomo paid the $6,000 due. Gem then sued Cuomo for an additional $300, and at the small claims court hearing testified that Cuomo had orally agreed to pay an additional $3 a dozen. The judge held the evidence inadmissible because (A) all contracts must be in writing to be enforceable, (B) written contracts may not be modified at the will of the parties, (C) a contract of guaranty must be in writing to be enforceable, (D) evidence of an oral agreement that contradicts a written contract is inadmissible.	________	2.______
3. Berry entered into an oral contract over the phone with a book club to purchase a book a month for $19.95 per book. After he had received and accepted one book, he decided to cancel the contract. Under this contract, Berry is liable for (A) the full contract price for one year, (B) none of the contract price, (C) $19.95, the cost of one book, (D) $39.90, the cost of two books.	________	3.______
4. The statute of frauds provides that a contract for the sale of goods costing $500 or more may be made orally if (A) the agreement is executory, (B) the buyer deposits at least $100, (C) the buyer receives and accepts the goods, (D) the goods are intangible.	________	4.______

ANSWERS SCORE

5. Lopez orally agreed to buy some computer equipment. When the company shipped the equipment, Lopez decided to accept and pay for only two items. Lopez is legally obligated to pay for (A) only the equipment he accepted, (B) all of the equipment he agreed to buy, (C) the equipment he accepted, plus half of the remainder of the order, (D) none of the equipment. ________ 5.______
6. Under the UCC, a sale of goods involves (A) real property, (B) real and personal property, (C) personal property, (D) items attached to real property only. ________ 6.______
7. A contract for the sale of goods that must be in writing according to the statute of frauds should be signed by (A) both parties, (B) only the seller, (C) only the buyer, (D) an outside third party. ________ 7.______
8. Marvin paid $600 cash for a color television at a local retail store. Marvin did not sign a memorandum for the sale. In this case, Marvin (A) can avoid the agreement because contracts for the sale of goods costing $500 or more must be in writing to be enforceable, (B) can avoid the agreement because a memorandum is required for all sales of merchandise, (C) cannot avoid the agreement because the contract need not be in writing when the buyer has paid in full for the goods, (D) cannot avoid the agreement because it involves specially manufactured goods. ________ 8.______
9. Fontane sold and delivered five copying machines to Durick according to the terms of their contract. Durick has a right to inspect the copiers before paying for them (A) unless the contract specified COD shipment, (B) only if Durick accepts delivery at Fontane's place of business, (C) only with permission from Fontane, (D) only if Durick notifies Fontane of the inspection. ________ 9.______
10. The buyer has a duty to accept goods and pay for them according to the terms of the contract (A) only if the goods are sent COD by the seller, (B) if there has been proper delivery and an inspection shows that the goods conform to the contract, (C) even after the goods have been rejected, (D) only for a cash sale. ________ 10.______

PART 3: Answer the following questions in the space provided. SCORE

1. A trail bike dealer in your town sells you a new trail bike. Under the UCC, would this be classified as a sale? Why or why not?

____

____

____ 1.______

2. A repair shop fixed the turntable on your stereo. Under the UCC, would this be classified as a sale? Why or why not?

____

____

____ 2.______

3. Lemond orally agreed to purchase three pairs of prescription eyeglasses for a total cost of $550. Can Lemond later claim that because the oral agreement involved goods costing more than $500, she is not bound by it?

____

____

____ 3.______

NAME ______________________________ DATE ______________

Activity—Analyzing a Sales Contract

Study the bill of sale shown below and then answer the questions on page 62.

BILL OF SALE

That Beverly B. Richards, a single person

of Marion *County, in the State of* Indiana *, has this day bargained and sold, and doeshereby bargain, sell, assign, transfer, set over, and deliver to* Herschel Clifford Simpson, a single person, *in* Marion *County, in the State of* Indiana *, for the sum of* One Thousand ($1,000.00)--- *Dollars, to* Beverly B. Richards *in hand paid, the receipt whereof is hereby acknowledged, the following described Chattels, Goods, and Personal Property in* Marion *County, State of* Indiana *, to-wit:*

One (1) antique cherry bedroom suite, consisting of bed, dresser, night stand, and mirror.

In Witness Whereof, *The said* Beverly B. Richards *has hereunto set* her *hand and seal this* 5th *day of* June *19* —

Signed, sealed, and delivered in presence of Beverly B. Richards .... *(Seal)*
Beverly B. Richards

.... *(Seal)*

.... *(Seal)*

1. Is the seller in this example a merchant or a nonmerchant? Why? SCORE

____

____

____ 1.______

2. Why is it necessary to know whether the seller is a merchant or a nonmerchant?

____

____

____ 2.______

3. Would this contract be enforceable if it had been made orally? Why or why not?

____

____

____ 3.______

4. What type of property is the subject of this sales contract?

____

____

____ 4.______

5. If the money paid for this property had been $10 instead of $1,000, could this contract be set aside because it was unconscionable? Explain your answer.

____

____

____ 5.______

UNIT 3 Purchase and Sale of Goods

Chapter 16 Title and Risk of Loss

NAME________________________________ DATE__________

SCORE__________

Study Guide and Review

PART 1: For each statement, write the letter of the best answer in the Answers column. *ANSWERS* *SCORE*

1. Goods that are not in existence and not yet identified are called (A) personal goods, (B) real goods, (C) future goods, (D) unsatisfactory goods. ________ 1.______
2. Mincer bought an electric saw from Brown's Hardware Store. Since the saw needed minor adjustments, he left it with the dealer. Risk of loss passed to Mincer (A) when Mincer made the agreement, (B) when Mincer picked up the saw, (C) when Mincer felt that the saw was satisfactory, (D) when Mincer accepted the risk of loss. ________ 2.______
3. Figmont, of Albany, New York, ordered 50 calculators from Mund Calculator Company, terms FOB Atlanta, Georgia. The calculators were damaged in transit from Atlanta to Albany. Who must suffer the loss? (A) Figmont, (B) Figmont and Mund Calculator equally, (C) Figmont suffers 25% and Mund 75%, (D) Mund Calculator. ________ 3.______
4. Lannigan bought an onyx ring and left it with the jeweler to be sized. Before it was sized, Tanzer came into the store to purchase an onyx ring. Since Lannigan's ring was the only onyx ring Tanzer liked, the jeweler sold it. Could Tanzer keep the ring? (A) Yes. A merchant who has temporary possession of goods can transfer a valid title. (B) Yes. A merchant who has temporary possession of goods can transfer a voidable title. (C) No. A buyer obtains no better title to goods than the seller. (D) No. A buyer with a voidable title cannot transfer a valid title. ________ 4.______
5. Barnes went to Caines Furniture Store to buy a sofa. The store was sold out, but agreed to order one for Barnes. This transaction is (A) a present sale, (B) void, (C) a contract to sell, (D) a sale of identified goods. ________ 5.______
6. If the requirements of the bulk transfer law are not met, creditors may have the right to declare a bulk sale (A) void, (B) voidable, (C) inadequate, (D) performed. ________ 6.______
7. Johnson bought a portable radio from Hughes without realizing that the radio was stolen. Johnson received (A) a valid title, (B) no title, (C) a voidable title, (D) an informal title. ________ 7.______
8. A bill of sale is (A) a storage document, (B) used in a ''sale or return,'' (C) written proof of ownership of goods, (D) a document that shows a person is keeping goods beyond the approval date. ________ 8.______
9. When he bought a new boat, Johnson was given the choice of delivery FOB shipping point or FOB destination. Of these terms, delivery FOB destination is to Johnson's legal advantage because (A) risk of loss passes to him when the boat is delivered to the carrier, (B) shipping expenses on the boat will be paid by the buyer upon delivery, (C) Johnson will not sustain the loss if the boat is damaged in transit, (D) all losses caused by damage to the boat will fall upon the carrier. ________ 9.______
10. Kim charged a lamp at the Ames Department Store and asked that it be delivered to her house on the next delivery run. If the lamp is damaged while being loaded onto the delivery truck, which statement best describes Kim's legal position: (A) the risk of loss has not yet shifted to Kim, so Ames must bear the loss of the lamp, (B) the risk of loss shifted to Kim at the moment the Ames employees were loading the lamp onto the truck, so Kim must now bear the loss, (C) Kim must accept delivery of the lamp even though it is damaged because she charged it, (D) Kim does not have to pay because the lamp is considered to be future goods. ________ 10.______

PART 2: For each of the following case problems, give a decision by writing "yes" or "no" in the space provided. Then, in sentence form, give a reason for your decision.

SCORE

1. Rogers ordered some electrical equipment from Cobb in Dayton, Ohio. The equipment was shipped to Utica, New York, terms FOB Utica. An accidental fire destroyed the equipment soon after it left Dayton. Must Rogers bear the loss in this case?

Decision: ______________________________

Reason: ______________________________

____

____

______________________________ 1.______

2. Gornig bought a dozen sport shirts from Rock's Men's Shop, paid for them, and asked the merchant to hold the shirts in the store until he could pick them up the next day. During the night, a fire destroyed the store and its contents. Gornig demanded return of his money, claiming that he had not yet taken physical possession of the shirts. Is Gornig entitled to a return of his money?

Decision: ______________________________

Reason: ______________________________

____

____

______________________________ 2.______

Activity—Analyzing a Bill of Sale

Read the bill of sale below and then answer the questions that follow.

SCORE

Know all Persons by these Presents, that I, Norton R. Galbraith of Cleveland, Ohio, for and in consideration of the sum of one thousand dollars ($1,000) in cash, paid to me by Robert McNit, of Ashland, Ohio, have sold to said Robert McNit the following: one used microcomputer.

In witness whereof, I have hereunto set my hand and seal this 10th day of December, 19—.

(signed) Norton R. Galbraith

Signed in the presence of: (signed) Frances Garner

1. Is this bill of sale formal or informal? ______________________________ 1.______
2. Who is the buyer? ______________________________ 2.______
3. Who is the seller? ______________________________ 3.______
4. Who was the witness to this bill of sale? ______________________________ 4.______
5. After the bill of sale was properly prepared, signed, and delivered, and the consideration exchanged, who was the legal owner of the microcomputer? ______________________________ 5.______

UNIT 3 Purchase and Sale of Goods

Chapter 17 Products Liability

NAME________________________ DATE____________

SCORE____________

Study Guide and Review

PART 1: Indicate whether each statement below is true or false by circling either "true" or "false" in the Answers column.

	ANSWERS		SCORE
1. The modern trend in court cases is to allow anyone harmed by a defective product to sue whoever is in any way responsible.	true	false	1.______
2. The Magnuson-Moss Warranty Act requires that all express warranties given by manufacturers be full warranties.	true	false	2.______
3. Products liability cases are all based upon breach of warranty.	true	false	3.______
4. Statements by salespersons expressing their opinions about the quality of the goods they sell constitute express warranties.	true	false	4.______
5. Even though it is not written, an implied warranty imposes obligations on a seller.	true	false	5.______
6. If a buyer purchases goods after inspecting a model, there is an implied warranty that the goods will conform to the model.	true	false	6.______
7. The implied warranty of merchantability may be excluded either orally or in writing.	true	false	7.______
8. Both merchants and nonmerchants can make implied warranties of fitness for a particular purpose.	true	false	8.______
9. Under the UCC, it is not necessary that a warranty be given at the time of sale.	true	false	9.______
10. In making an express warranty to a buyer, the seller does not have to actually use the word "warranty."	true	false	10.______

PART 2: For each statement, write the letter of the best answer in the Answers column.

	ANSWERS	SCORE
1. In selling an electronic game to a customer, the salesperson stated that "the game is made of a durable plastic and will not crack or break even when dropped on the floor." The salesperson's statement (A) is sales puffing, (B) is an implied warranty, (C) is an express warranty, (D) creates a warranty of merchantability.	________	1.______
2. Martins bought an automotive diagnostic analyzer for $59.95. A one-year warranty covering original factory defects in materials and workmanship came with the analyzer. The consideration given by Martins for the warranty was (A) part of the purchase price, (B) giving up the right to sue the store, (C) acceptance of the offer to buy the analyzer, (D) the entire sales contract.	________	2.______
3. "Products liability" describes the liability that manufacturers and sellers have to those harmed because of (A) products they place on the market that are defective or do not work right, (B) their lack of privity of contract, (C) their lack of negligence, (D) their lack of knowledge about warranties.	________	3.______
4. Montgomery cut her mouth on a piece of glass that was in a bowl of chili at Piper's Restaurant. If Montgomery sues the restaurant, she may base her action on (A) the express warranty of title, (B) the express warranty of description, (C) the implied warranty of merchantability, (D) the express warranty of merchantability.	________	4.______
5. Under the UCC, a warranty, oral or written, given by the seller following the sale (A) becomes part of the original sales contract without additional consideration, (B) must be accompanied by additional consideration, (C) is illegal, (D) is a breach of the sales contract.	________	5.______

PART 3: For each of the following case problems, give a decision by writing "yes" or "no" in the space provided. Then, in sentence form, give a reason for your decision.

SCORE

1. Mrs. Santos called "Chicken Delight" and ordered several buckets of chicken for a party. Following the party, two guests became seriously ill because some of the chicken was spoiled. The sick guests missed several days of work while they were under a doctor's care. Since they had used up their sick time, they were not paid for the days they missed. Could the guests sue "Chicken Delight" for damages resulting from their medical bills and their lost pay?

Decision: ______________________________

Reason: ______________________________

____

______________________________ 1. ______

2. Horton entered into a written contract to sell and install a central air conditioning system in Cordero's house. A week after the system was installed, Cordero asked Horton about a warranty, and Horton warranted the system in writing against all defects for one year. Eight months later, the system broke down because of a defective switch. Could Cordero enforce the warranty?

Decision: ______________________________

Reason: ______________________________

____

______________________________ 2. ______

3. When he ordered a water pump by mail, Banks specified that he wanted one that would pump 25 gallons a minute. When the pump arrived and was installed, Banks found that it pumped only 20 gallons a minute. Was there a breach of warranty?

Decision: ______________________________

Reason: ______________________________

____

______________________________ 3. ______

4. Sims bought a 50-amp battery charger from Newcomb. A short time later, Cole recognized the battery charger as one that had been stolen from him, and he took the charger back from Sims. When Sims demanded that Newcomb refund his money, Newcomb claimed that since he never stated that he had title to the charger, Sims had no rights against him. Is Newcomb legally correct?

Decision: ______________________________

Reason: ______________________________

____

______________________________ 4. ______

UNIT 3 Purchase and Sale of Goods

Chapter 18 Breach of Sales Contract

NAME________________________________ DATE__________

SCORE__________

Study Guide and Review

PART 1: Indicate whether each statement below is true or false by circling either "true" or "false" in the Answers column.

	ANSWERS		SCORE
1. The buyer may sue for breach of warranty only after notice is given to the seller.	true	false	1._____
2. An unpaid seller's lien is lost if the seller delivers possession of the goods to the buyer before discovering the buyer's insolvency.	true	false	2._____
3. Under the UCC, a breach of contract by one party allows the injured party to pursue more than one remedy.	true	false	3._____
4. If the seller breaches the contract, the buyer may demand that the seller deliver the goods in an action called "cover."	true	false	4._____
5. When a buyer breaches a sales contract, the seller may resell the goods at either a public auction or a private sale.	true	false	5._____
6. An unpaid seller who delivers goods to the buyer on credit and discovers that the buyer is unable to pay for them may reclaim the goods even if the buyer has resold them.	true	false	6._____
7. Demanding specific performance is a seller's remedy.	true	false	7._____
8. Generally, both the seller and the buyer meet their obligations as required by the sales contract.	true	false	8._____
9. Only consumers who buy from merchants have the right to "cover."	true	false	9._____
10. Damages sought by a buyer for a breach of the sales contract by the seller are determined by the difference between the contract price and the expenses connected with the breach.	true	false	10._____

PART 2: Answer each of the following questions in the space provided. **SCORE**

1. List three remedies available to the buyer if the seller breaches the sales contract.

____

____

____

____ 1._____

2. List three remedies available to the seller if the buyer breaches the sales contract.

____

____

____

____ 2._____

PART 3: For each statement, write the letter of the best answer in the Answers column. *ANSWERS* *SCORE*

1. If the seller learns that the buyer has become insolvent while the goods are in transit with a common carrier, the seller can exercise the right to (A) stop the goods in transit, (B) claim an unpaid seller's lien on the goods, (C) sue the buyer for fraud, (D) sue the buyer for conversion. ________ 1.______
2. Snyder sold some standard-sized sheets of plywood on credit to Robinson, promising delivery within 10 days. Five days later, Snyder wrongfully refused to deliver the goods to Robinson. Robinson, the buyer, is legally entitled to (A) sue for the purchase price, (B) exercise a right of lien on the goods, (C) sue for specific performance, (D) purchase similar goods elsewhere and sue for damages. ________ 2.______
3. Frances, owner of Best Buy Department Store, accepted and paid for 25 dozen ballpoint pens from the Perkins Stationery Company. After selling some of these pens, Frances began to get complaints that the pens would not write. What action can Frances take against the Perkins Company? (A) none, (B) resell the goods and sue for damages, (C) sue for specific performance, (D) sue Perkins for breach of warranty. ________ 3.______
4. A seller who is notified that the buyer will not go through with the contract may (A) cancel the contract, (B) obtain specific performance, (C) sue for breach of warranty, (D) cover. ________ 4.______
5. A remedy that is not available to a seller is to (A) rescind the contract, (B) reclaim the goods, (C) stop the goods in transit, (D) sue for breach of warranty. ________ 5.______

Activity—Scrambled Phrases

The scrambled phrases below represent remedies that sellers and buyers may pursue in the event of a breach by one party. Unscramble each phrase so that it forms the correct remedy. Then identify the remedy as that of the seller or of the buyer. *SCORE*

1. ODSOG NI OTSP NARSITT HTE ________________________________

   ________________________________ Remedied Party ________________ 1.______

2. UES NCACLE NAOTRCTC ORF HTE NAD ASGEADM ________________________________

   ________________________________ Remedied Party ________________ 2.______

3. EUS FO NAWYRATR OFR RAEBHC ________________________________

   ________________________________ Remedied Party ________________ 3.______

4. NTRTCACO ICSNERD HTE ________________________________

   ________________________________ Remedied Party ________________ 4.______

5. NAD NAECLC RUPAHCSE ETH VCEOR HET NCOATCRT ________________________________

   ________________________________ Remedied Party ________________ 5.______

6. NA ENLI PADINU XEECISRE LLESR'SE ________________________________

   ________________________________ Remedied Party ________________ 6.______

7. ODOGS ESLERL HET ________________________________ Remedied Party ________________ 7.______

UNIT 3 Purchase and Sale of Goods

Review

NAME________________________________ DATE__________

SCORE__________

Review

PART 1: Indicate whether each statement below is true or false by circling either "true" or "false" in the Answers column.

	ANSWERS		SCORE
1. Under the UCC, an agreement modifying a contract for the sale of goods needs no consideration to be binding.	true	false	1._____
2. When a merchant sells to a consumer at the merchant's place of business, risk of loss does not pass until the buyer actually receives the goods.	true	false	2._____
3. In a sale of goods FOB shipping point, risk of loss passes to the buyer when the goods are properly delivered to the carrier at the shipping point.	true	false	3._____
4. A buyer with a voidable title can transfer a valid title to a third party who obtained the goods for value and in good faith.	true	false	4._____
5. A sale or return is a present sale in which risk of loss passes to the buyer when the buyer accepts the goods by giving his or her approval.	true	false	5._____
6. Part of the purchase price of goods purchased under a sales contract is consideration for any express warranty given with those goods.	true	false	6._____
7. The warranty of title may be an express or an implied warranty.	true	false	7._____
8. Express warranties may not be excluded from sales contracts even if clear, specific language is used.	true	false	8._____
9. Under the UCC, courts may refuse to enforce an entire contract or any particular clause in a contract it finds unconscionable at the time the agreement was made.	true	false	9._____
10. A bill of sale may be an informal writing, such as a sales slip from a store, or it may be a formal document.	true	false	10._____

PART 2: For each statement, write the letter of the best answer in the Answers column.

	ANSWERS	SCORE
1. The bulk sales law pertains to (A) the sale of an entire stock of goods, outside the ordinary course of a merchant's business, to one person, (B) the sale of bulky goods, (C) the sale of land, (D) none of these answers.	________	1._____
2. Which statement made by a salesclerk at the time of a sale is a warranty: (A) "This coat is an unusual bargain." (B) "This coat will be in style for many years." (C) "This coat has an all-silk lining." (D) "This coat will wear like iron."	________	2._____
3. A warranty implied in every sale of goods is that (A) the goods are of high quality, (B) the seller has title to the goods, (C) the seller will refund the purchase price if the goods are unsatisfactory, (D) the purchase price is reasonable.	________	3._____
4. If the buyer possesses and holds title to goods but is found to be insolvent, within 10 days the seller may (A) place a lien on the goods, (B) reclaim the goods, (C) rescind the transfer of the title, (D) resell the goods to a third party.	________	4._____
5. If the buyer wrongfully refuses to accept goods when the seller makes proper delivery, the seller is legally entitled to (A) keep the goods for his own use and sue for the purchase price, (B) sue the buyer for damages for not accepting the goods, (C) sue the buyer for specific performance, (D) sue the buyer for breach of warranty.	________	5._____

ANSWERS SCORE

6. Young purchased a 50-foot length of garden hose at a hardware store. When she tried to use it, the hose pulled apart in several places. Was there any breach of warranty by the store? (A) Yes. There was an implied warranty that the goods were of the finest quality. (B) Yes. There was an implied warranty that the goods were merchantable. (C) No. No warranties were expressed by the store clerk. (D) No. Unless the store states a definite warranty, there is none in a sale. ________ 6.______
7. When goods are shipped from Buffalo, New York, to Columbus, Georgia, terms FOB Columbus, risk of loss passes to the buyer when the (A) contract is made, (B) goods are delivered to the common carrier, (C) goods reach their destination, (D) goods leave the seller's warehouse. ________ 7.______
8. The McCracken Garment Company sold 100 clown suits to Getz for $2,000. Getz inspected the goods and paid for 10 suits at the time of the sale. Getz later refused to receive and accept the rest of the suits, claiming that since the goods cost over $500, the oral agreement was unenforceable. Can Getz get his money back for the 10 suits he paid for, even though the contract was oral? (A) Yes. There was no written memorandum of the sale. (B) No. Acceptance of the 10 clown suits makes the entire agreement enforceable. (C) Yes. The agreement was unenforceable under the statute of frauds. (D) No. When the buyer has made part payment, the contract can be enforced for those goods covered by the partial payment. ________ 8.______
9. Goods not yet in existence and not yet identified are called (A) non-existing goods, (B) real goods, (C) future goods, (D) personal goods. ________ 9.______
10. Unless a contract for the sale of a stereo states otherwise, the place of delivery is the (A) seller's residence, (B) buyer's residence, (C) buyer's place of business, (D) seller's place of business. ________ 10.______

PART 3: For each of the following case problems, give a decision by writing "yes" or "no" in the space provided. Then, in sentence form, give a reason for your decision.

SCORE

1. Briggs wanted to buy a computer for his home-based business. He went to the Harvard Computer Supply Company and signed a written memorandum to purchase one for $2500. However, Briggs refused to accept delivery of the computer the next day, saying he had changed his mind. He claimed that the memorandum he signed was not enforceable because the salesperson had not signed it. Is Briggs liable for breach of contract?

Decision: ____

Reason: ____

____

____ 1.______

2. Friske, of Boston, Massachusetts, placed an order with Kevin Supply Company in Dayton, Ohio, for office furniture according to a description given in a catalog. If, after the furniture is received in Boston, Friske finds that it does not conform to the description in the catalog, does he have a legal claim against the Kevin Supply Company?

Decision: ____

Reason: ____

____

____ 2.______

NAME ______________________________ DATE ______________

SCORE

3. In the case described in Number 2, the shipping terms were FOB Dayton. If the furniture is damaged enroute to Boston, through no fault of the common carrier, should Friske bear the loss?

Decision: ______________________________

Reason: ______________________________

____

____

______________________________ 3. ______

4. Jayson purchased a power lawnmower from the American Department Store, terms ''on 30-day approval.'' Before the 30-day period had expired, a thief broke into Jayson's garage and stole the mower. Must Jayson bear the loss in this case?

Decision: ______________________________

Reason: ______________________________

____

____

______________________________ 4. ______

PART 4: Answer the following questions in the space provided.

1. Compare the three theories of liability that a buyer who is injured may use in a products liability action. How do these theories differ?

____

____

____

____

____

____

____

____

____

____

______________________________ 1. ______

2. Explain why it is difficult for a merchant to completely avoid making any type of express warranty. SCORE

____

____

____

____

____

____

____

____

____ 2.______

PART 5: Base your answers to questions 1 through 5 on the following information. ANSWERS SCORE

McDonnell purchased an electric razor from the Sibley Department Store for $79.95. He took the razor home when he made the sales agreement on December 10, and he paid for the razor at the end of the 30-day credit period. The following statement appeared on a tag attached to the razor:

LIMITED WARRANTY

Warranted for one year from the date of purchase against original factory imperfections in materials and workmanship. During this time, Excello will elect to repair or replace the product without charge for parts or labor, provided the product is returned to the manufacturer with the warranty card. Excello Razor Company

1. The warranty statement on the tag represents an (A) express warranty, (B) implied warranty, (C) express and an implied warranty, (D) exclusion of warranties. ________ 1.______
2. McDonnell would benefit from the warranty if (A) he left the razor out in the rain on a camping trip and the razor was damaged, (B) he gave the razor to a friend for Christmas and the friend did not like it enough to use it, (C) the cutting edges of the razor became dull after McDonnell used it for one month, (D) the razor did not give him as good a shave as his old razor. ________ 2.______
3. The consideration given by McDonnell for the warranty was (A) his reputation, (B) his acceptance of the electric razor, (C) part of the purchase price, (D) money paid in addition to the purchase price. ________ 3.______
4. McDonnell brought the razor back for an adjustment two weeks after he bought it. He questioned the clerk about the razor's quality. The clerk replied that in addition to the manufacturer's warranty, the store guaranteed all razors for two years against all defects, and if necessary would replace the razor with a new one. This statement is (A) binding, because a warranty made after a sales contract is completed needs no additional consideration, (B) binding, because it is based on common usage in the trade, and most razors carry such a guarantee, (C) not binding, because it is based on past consideration, (D) not binding, because it represents mere sales talk or "puffing." ________ 4.______
5. Risk of loss passed to McDonnell (A) January 10, (B) December 10, (C) January 9, (D) December 11. ________ 5.______

UNIT 4 CONSUMER PROTECTION

Chapter 19 A Bill of Rights for the Consumer

NAME________________________________ DATE__________

SCORE__________

Study Guide and Review

PART 1: Indicate whether each statement below is true or false by circling either "true" or "false" in the Answers column.

	ANSWERS		SCORE
1. The U.S. Department of Commerce is the agency primarily responsible for enforcing consumer rights.	true	false	1._____
2. Failure to disclose important information may be considered false advertising.	true	false	2._____
3. The manufacturer's name and address do not have to appear on cosmetics labels.	true	false	3._____
4. Price fixing violates both state and federal laws.	true	false	4._____
5. Government agencies have the power to enforce safety standards as well as to set them.	true	false	5._____
6. A person who receives unordered goods must either return them or throw them away.	true	false	6._____
7. The Federal Trade Commission may require advertisements for certain products to carry warnings about their use.	true	false	7._____
8. All contracts must now be written in "plain" English.	true	false	8._____
9. Violation of a consumer protection law is a criminal offense only.	true	false	9._____
10. You do not have to give a reason for canceling a purchase from a door-to-door salesperson.	true	false	10._____

PART 2: Answer the following questions in the space provided. SCORE

1. List four consumer rights and give an example of each.

____

____

____

____

____

____ 1._____

2. List three federal consumer ageneies and describe their functions.

____

____

____

____ 2._____

PART 3: For each of the following case problems, give a decision by writing "yes" or "no" in the space provided. Then, in sentence form, give a reason for your answer. *SCORE*

1. Acme Supermarket and Peach Supermarket agreed to charge the same prices for their fruits and vegetables, resulting in a lower price for consumers. Have these supermarkets violated the law?

   Decision: ______________________________

   Reason: ______________________________

   ______________________________ 1. ______

2. Turner bought a new TV from a department store, paying for it in cash. Two days later, she tried to return it, claiming she had a right to rescind the sales contract within three days of the purchase. Is Turner correct?

   Decision: ______________________________

   Reason: ______________________________

   ______________________________ 2. ______

PART 4: Look at the product shown below. In the spaces provided at the right, describe violations of the consumer labeling laws. *SCORE*

______________________________ 1. ______

______________________________ 2. ______

______________________________ 3. ______

______________________________ 4. ______

PART 5: Assume that your state has a "plain English" law. Read the following clause from an actual lease and rewrite it in "plain English." *SCORE*

"The landlord hereinabove named does hereby let unto the tenant hereinabove named, the premises known as 422 Cole Street, Cole, Ohio, for the term of two years commencing January 1. The tenant hereby agrees to take said premises for the aforesaid term under the terms and conditions hereinafter described."

____

____

____

______________________________ ______

UNIT 4 CONSUMER PROTECTION

Chapter 20 A Bill of Rights for the Borrower

NAME ______________________________ DATE __________

SCORE __________

Study Guide and Review

PART 1: For each statement, write the letter of the best answer in the Answers column. *ANSWERS* *SCORE*

1. Discrimination in granting credit is prohibited by the (A) Federal Trade Act, (B) Commerce Act, (C) Equal Credit Opportunity Act, (D) Fair Credit Act. ________ 1. ______
2. In deciding whether to grant credit, a creditor may consider an applicant's (A) religion, (B) geographical residence, (C) income, (D) marital status. ________ 2. ______
3. In deciding whether to grant credit, a creditor may refuse to consider income from (A) alimony, (B) pension, (C) part-time employment, (D) gambling. ________ 3. ______
4. The amount of money paid for the use of credit is the (A) annual charge, (B) finance charge, (C) borrowing fee, (D) percentage fee. ________ 4. ______
5. A person whose credit card is stolen and who notifies the card issuer of the theft is liable for charges made with the card up to (A) the total amount charged, (B) $100, (C) $250, (D) $50. ________ 5. ______
6. An incorrect bill received by a consumer must be corrected within (A) 30 days, (B) 45 days, (C) 60 days, (D) 90 days. ________ 6. ______
7. A consumer who believes a bill is incorrect must notify the (A) Federal Trade Commission, (B) Better Business Bureau, (C) creditor, (D) Chamber of Commerce. ________ 7. ______
8. Assets of a debtor that may not be taken to satisfy a judgment include (A) a car, (B) a bank account, (C) stocks, (D) household furniture. ________ 8. ______
9. Usury laws generally do not apply to (A) credit card charges, (B) mortgage loans, (C) education loans, (D) vacation loans. ________ 9. ______
10. A person may file for bankruptcy (A) once a year, (B) once in a lifetime, (C) every twelve years, (D) every six years. ________ 10. ______

PART 2: Indicate whether each statement is true or false by circling either "true" or "false" in the Answers column. *ANSWERS* *SCORE*

1. Lenders may refuse credit to someone who is receiving public assistance. true false 1. ______
2. Creditors may always consider a potential borrower's age in determining whether to grant credit. true false 2. ______
3. A lender must disclose the finance charge, but not the annual percentage rate. true false 3. ______
4. The law does not require that service or carrying charges added to the finance charges be disclosed to the borrower. true false 4. ______
5. If you lose a credit card because of your negligence, you may be held responsible for an unlimited amount of unauthorized charges. true false 5. ______
6. A person who is denied credit is entitled to know the reasons for having a credit application rejected. true false 6. ______
7. A consumer who believes a bill is incorrect does not have to make any payment on the bill until the error is corrected. truc false 7. ______
8. An agreement requiring an interest rate higher than the contract rate is usurious. true false 8. ______
9. After being discharged in bankruptcy, a bankrupt is no longer responsible for any debts. true false 9. ______
10. When the interest rate is not stated in a loan or credit agreement, the maximum that may be charged is known as the legal rate. true false 10. ______

PART 3: For each of the following case problems, give a decision by writing "yes" or "no" in the space provided. Then, in sentence form, give a reason for your answer.

SCORE

1. Garnett needed capital to expand her business. She found a friend who agreed to lend her the money at 25% interest per year. When Garnett failed to pay the debt, her friend sued. Garnett claimed that the loan was invalid because the maximum interest rate in her state is 12%. Is Garnett legally correct?

Decision: ______________________________

Reason: ______________________________

____

______________________________ 1. ______

2. Briggs discovered that her debts exceeded her assets by a considerable amount, and she could not pay her bills on time. Is bankruptcy the only solution?

Decision: ______________________________

Reason: ______________________________

____

______________________________ 2. ______

Activity 1—Word Search

The 10 words listed below describe important terms relating to consumer protection. The words read forward, backward, up, down, and diagonally, but always in a straight line and never skipping letters. Circle each word you find.

SCORE

U	B	A	I	H	T	I	D	E	R	C	C
S	A	M	N	U	I	N	S	B	O	R	H
A	N	L	S	Y	N	S	M	A	H	E	R
R	K	Y	O	R	O	T	B	E	D	D	I
E	R	T	L	U	G	A	N	T	A	I	L
W	U	K	V	S	D	L	D	E	N	T	O
O	P	A	E	U	G	L	M	L	F	O	U
R	T	L	N	Z	E	M	C	E	K	R	R
R	C	E	C	L	K	E	X	E	M	P	T
O	Y	X	Y	P	S	N	O	C	I	V	C
B	K	L	A	R	E	T	A	L	L	O	C

bankruptcy
borrower
collateral
credit
creditor
debtor
exempt
insolvency
installment
usury

______

UNIT 4 CONSUMER PROTECTION

Chapter 21 A Bill of Rights for the Creditor

NAME________________________________ DATE__________

SCORE__________

Study Guide and Review

PART 1: Answer each question below by circling "yes" or "no" in the Answers column.

	ANSWERS		*SCORE*
1. To be collectible, must a debt always be in writing?	yes	no	1.______
2. May an unsecured creditor repossess the item for which credit was given?	yes	no	2.______
3. May a creditor refuse to give credit unless security is given?	yes	no	3.______
4. Is a secured loan valid if a financing statement is not filed?	yes	no	4.______
5. May a secured creditor repossess the collateral without going to court?	yes	no	5.______
6. Is a guarantor primarily responsible for paying the debtor's obligation?	yes	no	6.______
7. If the debtor and creditor change the interest rate on a guaranteed loan, is the guarantor freed of all responsibility on the loan?	yes	no	7.______
8. May a taxing authority sell someone's property if that person fails to pay the taxes?	yes	no	8.______
9. If a secured creditor repossesses property and decides to sell it, must the sale be public?	yes	no	9.______
10. Does a financing statement protect the creditor as well as the public?	yes	no	10.______

PART 2: Read the case problem below and then in the space provided answer the questions. *SCORE*

Granby wanted to borrow money from Public Bank to purchase a new car. Since Granby's credit was poor, Public Bank agreed to lend the money to Granby only if Granby's brother would act as guarantor. Granby and his brother signed the contract.

1. If Granby defaults in paying the loan, what are Public Bank's remedies?

____

____ 1.______

2. If Public repossesses the car, may it sell the car at a private sale? ______________________ 2.______

3. If Granby defaults on the loan, must Public first try to collect from Granby before trying to collect from his brother?

____ 3.______

4. If Granby does not pay, can Public hold his brother liable for making the payment? Explain your answer.

____

____

____ 4.______

5. If Granby's brother was a surety rather than a guarantor, would this make a difference? Explain your answer.

____

____ 5.______

PART 3: In the Answers column at the right, write the letter of the word or words from Column 1 that best match each item in Column 2.

COLUMN 1	COLUMN 2	ANSWERS	SCORE
(A) surety	1. A notice that a security interest no longer exists	______	1.____
(B) collateral	2. The act of taking back property that is subject to a security agreement.	______	2.____
(C) financing statement	3. A person who promises to repay a debt if the debtor fails to do so after attempts are made to collect from the debtor.	______	3.____
(D) guarantor	4. A secured interest in property granted by law.	______	4.____
(E) lien	5. Property subject to a security interest.	______	5.____
(F) termination statement	6. A public notice of a security interest.	______	6.____
(G) repossession	7. A person who promises to repay the obligation of a debtor even though the creditor does not first attempt to collect from the debtor.	______	7.____
(H) judgment lien	8. A lien for those who supply labor, materials, or services in the construction of buildings.	______	8.____
(I) creditors' bill of rights	9. Statutes provided to creditors to ensure payment.	______	9.____
(J) mechanic's lien	10. A lien granted to a creditor who has sued a debtor.	______	10.____

PART 4: Answer the following questions in the space provided. SCORE

1. Assume that you operate a piano store. A customer wants to buy a piano and pay for it by making a small deposit and paying the balance over three years.

   a. What methods could you use to make sure that you receive the balance?

   ____

   ____

   ______________________________ 1a.____

   b. If the customer is not able to make any payments after three months, what options do you have?

   ____

   ____

   ______________________________ 1b.____

2. List and explain three different types of liens used to protect a creditor's interest.

   ____

   ____

   ____

   ____

   ____

   ______________________________ 2.____

UNIT 4 CONSUMER PROTECTION

Review

NAME______________________________ DATE__________

SCORE__________

Review

PART 1: In the Answers column at the right, write the letter of the word or words in Column 1 that best match each statement in Column 2.

COLUMN 1	*COLUMN 2*	*ANSWERS*	*SCORE*
(A) loss leader	1. The right to pay for goods and services after they have been received.	______	1.______
(B) collateral	2. An agreement between debtor and creditor that creates a security interest.	______	2.______
(C) security agreement	3. A lien given to those who supply materials, labor, and services in constructing buildings.	______	3.______
(D) consumer	4. Advertising designed to get a consumer to select a more expensive product than the one advertised.	______	4.______
(E) insolvency	5. An item sold at or below cost to attract customers.	______	5.______
(F) class action suit	6. Any type of asset that may be pledged as security to a bank or other creditor.	______	6.______
(G) bait and switch	7. Inability of a debtor to pay debts as they are due.	______	7.______
(H) mechanic's lien	8. A person who buys goods, products, and services.	______	8.______
(I) credit	9. A creditor who has a secured interest in property belonging to the debtor.	______	9.______
(J) secured creditor	10. An action that is taken by a consumer on behalf of a group of consumers.	______	10.______

PART 2: Indicate whether the following statements are true or false by circling "true" or "false" in the Answers column.

	ANSWERS		*SCORE*
1. Bait-and-switch advertising is permissible as long as the recommended item is superior to the item the consumer intended to buy.	true	false	1.______
2. Price fixing is a violation of both state and federal laws.	true	false	2.______
3. Failure to use "plain English" in a contract as required by law would make the contract voidable at the purchaser's or buyer's option.	true	false	3.______
4. Consumer rights may be enforced by groups as well as by individuals.	true	false	4.______
5. A lender may refuse to grant credit to a potential borrower solely because of that person's marital status.	true	false	5.______
6. The government may ban the sale of any product considered dangerous.	true	false	6.______
7. In deciding whether to grant credit, a creditor can discount the importance of income from alimony, part-time work, or a pension.	true	false	7.______
8. A security agreement is effective only if it is filed.	true	false	8.______
9. A secured creditor who repossesses property and decides to sell it must dispose of it at a public sale.	true	false	9.______
10. A secured creditor may usually repossess collateral without having to first resort to court procedures.	true	false	10.______

PART 3: For each statement, write the letter of the best answer in the Answers column. | *ANSWERS* | *SCORE*

1. Consumer protection laws have been enacted at (A) the state level, (B) the county level, (C) state and federal levels, (D) regional levels. ________ 1.______
2. If a retailer runs out of an advertised item, it must give a consumer (A) a credit, (B) an item of equal value, (C) a refund, (D) a rain check. ________ 2.______
3. Mislabeling an item with an incorrect "suggested retail price" is an example of (A) price fixing, (B) price misrepresentation, (C) bait-and-switch advertising, (D) a loss leader. ________ 3.______
4. A buyer's right to cancel a contract made with a door-to-door salesperson is guaranteed by (A) the Federal Trade Act, (B) the Truth in Lending Act, (C) the Unordered Goods Act, (D) the Return of Merchandise Act. ________ 4.______
5. A seller who violates consumer protection laws may be subject to (A) civil penalties, (B) criminal penalties, (C) both civil and criminal penalties, (D) none of these answers. ________ 5.______
6. The Smyth Company began to manufacture and sell a power lawnmower that had a tendency to catch on fire. The federal government may protect the public by (A) forcing a recall of the mowers, (B) requiring corrective action, (C) ordering a refund, (D) all of these answers. ________ 6.______
7. An unsecured debt (A) must be oral, (B) must be in writing, (C) may be either oral or written, (D) must be written and filed in the county clerk's office. ________ 7.______
8. An unsecured creditor may collect a debt by (A) seizing the item sold, (B) bringing suit to collect, (C) obtaining an injunction, (D) all of these answers. ________ 8.______
9. A secured creditor may collect a debt by (A) seizing the item and selling it, (B) bringing criminal charges against the debtor, (C) having the debtor arrested, (D) all of these answers. ________ 9.______
10. A security agreement is filed to (A) protect the debtor, (B) protect the public, (C) protect the creditor, (D) protect the creditor and the public. ________ 10.______
11. Collateral for a security interest (A) may be tangible or intangible personal property, (B) must be intangible personal property, (C) must be tangible personal property, (D) may be real property. ________ 11.______
12. In a secured transaction, collateral (A) must be in the debtor's possession, (B) must be in the creditor's possession, (C) may not be required, (D) may be in either the debtor's or the creditor's possession. ________ 12.______
13. Whether a person is a surety or a guarantor depends on (A) the purpose of the loan, (B) the interest rate of the loan, (C) who is primarily responsible for payment, (D) the age of the borrower. ________ 13.______
14. Anderson supplied bricks to a contractor to construct an apartment house. If the contractor does not pay for the bricks, Anderson will be protected by filing (A) a tax lien, (B) a debtor's lien, (C) a mechanic's lien, (D) a judgment lien. ________ 14.______
15. A secured creditor who repossesses the collateral when the debt is not paid (A) must sell it, (B) may keep it or sell it, (C) must deliver it to the police, (D) must return it to the debtor. ________ 15.______
16. A debtor may file a bankruptcy petition (A) every 2 years, (B) once a year, (C) every 6 years, (D) every 6 months. ________ 16.______
17. Collecting interest in excess of the legal rate is (A) price fixing, (B) legal, (C) price misrepresentation, (D) usury. ________ 17.______
18. If you receive an incorrect bill, you (A) need not pay it, (B) must notify the creditor, (C) must notify the Better Business Bureau, (D) may sue the creditor. ________ 18.______
19. A person who is denied credit is entitled to know (A) the name of the credit bureau supplying the credit report, (B) the address of the credit bureau, (C) the names of persons asking for credit reports, (D) all of these answers. ________ 19.______
20. If your credit card is stolen and you notify the card issuer, your liability is limited to (A) $100, (B) $75, (C) $50, (D) $500. ________ 20.______

NAME______________________________ DATE______________

Activity—Using Credit

Shown below is a retail installment credit contract. Read the contract and then answer the questions on the following page.

A-1 AUTOS 121 S. MAIN STREET, AKRON, OH 44308

RETAIL INSTALLMENT CONTRACT

Date: Sept. 25 19 --

Buyer's Name (Print): Marguerita Santos

Address: 207 E. Buchtel Avenue, Akron, OH 44325

The undersigned Seller hereby sells and the undersigned Buyer, having been quoted both the following Cash Price and the following Deferred Payment Price, hereby buys for the Deferred Payment Price, on the terms and conditions hereinafter set forth, the following described motor vehicle, with accessories and equipment thereon, receipt and acceptance of which, in satisfactory condition, are hereby acknowledged by Buyer:

NEW OR USED	YEAR	MAKE	BODY STYLE	MODEL NO.	NO. CYL.	FACTORY OR SERIAL #
Used	1982	Chev.	2-door	8-046	4	AL27884625

Special Accessories and Equipment
(Check or specify those applicable)

Transmission: ☐ Automatic ☑ 4-Speed

☐ Power Steering ☑ Power Brakes ☐ Power Windows

☐ Air-Conditioning ☑ Radio ☐ Other (Specify) ________

1. Cash Price (incl. taxes, accessories, services) $ 1200
2. Downpayment
   Cash Downpayment $ 200
   Trade-in $ -

   Yr. Model Make Serial #
   Total Downpayment $ 200
3. Unpaid Balance of Cash Price (1-2) $ 1000
4. Other Charges
   Certificate of Title Fee $ 10
   Registration Fee $ 25
   Optional Insurance $ -
5. Unpaid Balance Amount Financed (3 + 4) $ 1035
6. **Finance Charge** $ 93.15
7. Total of Payments (5 + 6) $ 1128.15
8. Deferred Payment Price (1 + 4 + 6) $ 1328.15

   Annual Percentage Rate 9%

PAYMENT SCHEDULE

Buyer hereby agrees to pay to Seller the Total of Payments (Item 7 from above) in 23 monthly installments of $ 47.00 each and one final installment of $47.00 on the like day of each month commencing Oct. 1, 19 -- or, if different from date of transaction, finance charge begins to accrue Oct. 1, 19 --.

Signed Marguerita Santos Date: 9/25/--

Signed ______________________ Date: __________

SCORE

1. What is the purchase price of the car? ____________ 1. ____

2. What are the total interest charges? ____________ 2. ____

3. What is the total cost of the car? ____________ 3. ____

4. Since items obviously end up costing more when they are bought on credit, what are the advantages of buying on credit?

____

____

____

____________ 4. ____

5. What are the disadvantages of buying on credit?

____

____

____

____________ 5. ____

6. With passage of the Truth in Lending Law, businesses providing credit to consumers were required to provide complete information on the cost of using credit. Write a short paragraph explaining how this law has helped consumers in making wiser buying decisions.

____

____

____

____

____

____

____

____

____

____

____

____________ 6. ____

UNIT 5 BAILMENTS

Chapter 22 Bailments of Personal Property

NAME________________________________ DATE__________

SCORE__________

Study Guide and Review

PART 1: Read each statement to determine whether it is an example of a bailment. Indicate your answer by circling either "yes" or "no" in the Answers column.

	ANSWERS		*SCORE*
1. You buy a bicycle, agreeing to pay for it over a two-year period.	yes	no	1.______
2. You lend your sister a tennis racket that you borrowed from a friend.	yes	no	2.______
3. A friend lets you use a tape recorder in the basement of his home.	yes	no	3.______
4. Your cousin lets you use her cottage for the weekend.	yes	no	4.______
5. A friend asks you to take his snowmobile in for repairs.	yes	no	5.______
6. A neighbor leaves a raincoat on the back seat of your car without telling you about it.	yes	no	6.______
7. A neighbor asks you to watch his child while he is in the store.	yes	no	7.______
8. You accept delivery of a television set on behalf of a friend who is away.	yes	no	8.______
9. You see someone else's wallet on the ground but do not pick it up.	yes	no	9.______
10. You store a radio and some clothing in a rented locker at a bus station.	yes	no	10.______
11. You place some jewelry and legal documents in a safety deposit box at a bank.	yes	no	11.______
12. Your friend keeps your guitar for you while you go on vacation.	yes	no	12.______
13. You ask a salesperson in a store to watch your coat while you go to a different department in the store.	yes	no	13.______
14. You find a briefcase that has been stolen and attempt to return it to its owner.	yes	no	14.______
15. You borrow a library book and agree to return it in two weeks.	yes	no	15.______

PART 2: Answer the questions below in the space provided. *SCORE*

1. List and briefly explain four characteristics of a valid bailment.

____

____

____

____

____ 1.______

2. Give two examples of bailments you have entered into. Do not use the ones mentioned in the text.

____

____

____ 2.______

PART 3: For each statement, write the letter of the best answer in the Answers column. *ANSWERS* *SCORE*

1. A bailment involves transfer of (A) title to, but not possession of, personal property, (B) title to, but not possession of, real property, (C) possession of, but not title to, personal property, (D) possession of, but not title to, real property. ________ 1.______
2. A bailment that arises because of the acts of the parties, without any oral or written agreement, is (A) illegal, (B) a bailment implied by law, (C) an express bailment, (D) a bailment implied in fact. ________ 2.______
3. Bailments implied by law are often created (A) through express agreements, (B) through implied agreements, (C) through mutual agreement, (D) when people find and take possession of lost or stolen property. ________ 3.______
4. If bailed property is lost or damaged as a result of the bailee's negligence, (A) the bailee has no liability, (B) the bailee is liable to the bailor for the value of the property, (C) the bailment is ended by mutual agreement, (D) the bailment is ended by operation of law. ________ 4.______
5. All of the following may be the subject of a bailment except (A) a stock certificate, (B) an automobile, (C) a garage, (D) a motorcycle. ________ 5.______

PART 4: In the Answers column at the right, write the word or expression that makes each statement correct. *ANSWERS* *SCORE*

1. A person who gets possession of a bailed item is the ______. ________________ 1.______
2. Only ______ property may be the subject of a bailment. ________________ 2.______
3. The transfer of personal property for a specific time and purpose is known as ______. ________________ 3.______
4. Land and buildings are examples of ______ property. ________________ 4.______
5. A bailment in which the agreement is stated in words, either oral or written, is an ______ agreement. ________________ 5.______

PART 5: Answer the questions below in the space provided. *SCORE*

1. Explain the difference between a bailment and a sale.

____

____ 1.______

2. Explain why depositing money in a bank is not considered a bailment.

____

____ 2.______

3. List five ways a bailment ends.

____

____

____

____ 3.______

UNIT 5 BAILMENTS

Chapter 23 Types of Bailments

NAME________________________ DATE__________

SCORE__________

Study Guide and Review

PART 1: In the Answers column at the right, write the word "true" if the statement is true. If the underlined word or words make the statement false, substitute the word or words needed to make the statement true.

	ANSWERS	*SCORE*
1. A mutual benefit bailment is one in which both parties benefit.	______	1.____
2. When only one party to a bailment benefits, it is known as a constructive bailment.	______	2.____
3. The standard of care required in a mutual benefit bailment is extraordinary care.	______	3.____
4. A bailee who is not paid for work done may exercise a bailee's lien.	______	4.____
5. A deposit of personal property as security for a loan is known as a pledge.	______	5.____
6. Special bailments require a reasonable degree of care.	______	6.____
7. Storing your friend's tractor as a favor is an example of an implied bailment.	______	7.____
8. Receiving goods on approval for purchase is an example of a pledge.	______	8.____
9. A bailment for the sole benefit of the bailor is a gratuitous bailment.	______	9.____
10. A person who gets possession of someone else's property by mistake has a bailment by necessity.	______	10.____

PART 2: Answer the following questions in the space provided. *SCORE*

1. List the five types of mutual benefit bailments. Give an example of each, but do not use the examples in the textbook.

____

____

____

____

____ 1.____

2. Give two examples of gratuitous bailments. Do not use the examples in the textbook.

____

____

____ 2.____

PART 3: In the Answers column at the right, write the letter of the word or words in Column 1 that best match each item in Column 2.

COLUMN 1	COLUMN 2	ANSWERS	SCORE
(A) consignment	1. A bailee's rights, before being paid, in the property bailed.	________	1. ______
(B) pledgor	2. A bailment that occurs when property comes into someone's possession by mistake.	________	2. ______
(C) high degree of care	3. The person who delivers personal property to a bailee.	________	3. ______
(D) warehouse receipt	4. The bailor in a consignment.	________	4. ______
(E) bailment by necessity	5. One who transfers property to make a pledge.	________	5. ______
(F) slight care	6. A receipt given by one who stores goods for another.	________	6. ______
(G) consignor	7. The bailee in a consignment.	________	7. ______
(H) bailee's lien	8. The degree of care required of a bailee in a bailment solely for the bailor's benefit.	________	8. ______
(I) consignee	9. A bailment for the purpose of purchase or sale by the bailee.	________	9. ______
(J) bailor	10. The degree of care required of a bailee in a bailment for the sole benefit of the bailee.	________	10. ______

PART 4: In each of the following case problems, give a decision by writing "yes" or "no" in the space provided. Then, in sentence form, give a reason for your decision.

SCORE

1. Sloan was going on vacation and asked Brown to keep his guitar while he was away. While Sloan was away, excessive humidity warped the guitar's neck and ruined it. When Sloan returned, he insisted that Brown pay him for the damaged guitar. Is he entitled to collect?

Decision: ____

Reason: ____

____

____ 1. ______

2. Monteiro, a high school senior, placed a camera in his high school locker and locked the door. When he returned from class, he discovered that the door had been broken and the camera stolen. Can he hold the school authorities liable for the loss?

Decision: ____

Reason: ____

____

____ 2. ______

3. By mistake, you receive in the mail a book ordered by your neighbor. Not wanting to be bothered by it, you leave it on your front porch. Two months later, the book is stolen. Are you liable to your neighbor for the loss?

Decision: ____

Reason: ____

____ 3. ______

UNIT 5 BAILMENTS

Chapter 24 Special Bailments

NAME____________________ DATE__________

SCORE__________

Study Guide and Review

PART 1: For each statement, write the letter of the best answer in the Answers column. *ANSWERS* *SCORE*

1. An example of a special bailment is the liability imposed on a (A) renter of a car, (B) trucking company, (C) parking garage, (D) auto service station. ______ 1.______
2. The degree of care imposed on a special bailee is (A) reasonable care, (B) slight care, (C) great care, (D) extraordinary care. ______ 2.______
3. Under common law, the liability of special bailees was (A) absolute, (B) minimal, (C) based on the status of the parties, (D) based on the property bailed. ______ 3.______
4. A special bailee's liability may be limited because of any of the following *except* (A) an act of God, (B) agreement between the bailor and the bailee, (C) acts of rioters, (D) acts of public authorities. ______ 4.______
5. A special bailee is not liable for losses resulting from a typhoon because (A) a typhoon is a natural disaster that the bailee could not have anticipated, (B) special bailments require only a reasonable level of care, (C) special bailees are exempt from all liabilities, (D) special bailees always have agreements with bailors to limit liability. ______ 5.______
6. A person who enters a hotel solely for the purpose of having dinner is a (A) hotel guest, (B) transient, (C) bailor by implication, (D) business guest. ______ 6.______
7. A hotelkeeper may refuse to accept a person as a guest because of that person's (A) inability to pay, (B) religion, (C) race, (D) sex. ______ 7.______
8. A carrier that transports goods for certain customers only is a (A) limited carrier, (B) common carrier, (C) contract carrier, (D) mutual carrier. ______ 8.______
9. The liability of a common carrier is that of a (A) special bailee, (B) ordinary bailee, (C) constructive bailee, (D) bailee by necessity. ______ 9.______
10. A common carrier whose equipment is detained by a customer for an unreasonable period of time may make a special charge known as (A) containerage, (B) detonage, (C) bailee's charge, (D) demurrage. ______ 10.______

PART 2: In the space below, list four exceptions to the rule of absolute liability of hotelkeepers and common carriers. Give an example of each exception. *SCORE*

1. ____

____ 1.______

2. ____

____ 2.______

3. ____

____ 3.______

4. ____

____ 4.______

PART 3: Read the following cases and answer the questions by circling either "yes" or "no" in the Answers column. State the rule of law that supports your answer. *ANSWERS* *SCORE*

1. Berger checked into a motel and left a valuable stamp collection in his room because the motel did not provide safe-deposit boxes. If the stamps are stolen, is the motel liable for the value of the collection? yes no

   Rule of law ______________________________

   ______________________________ 1. ______

2. Corrida Corporation shipped a large quantity of gold bars via Ajax Trucking Lines. The shipment was hijacked by a gang of escaped prisoners. Can Corrida hold Ajax responsible for the loss? yes no

   Rule of law ______________________________

   ______________________________ 2. ______

3. Thruston moved to a nearby city to start a new job. She rented a suite in a hotel for a two-year period. Would the hotelkeeper be absolutely liable to Thruston if any of her belongings were stolen? yes no

   Rule of law ______________________________

   ______________________________ 3. ______

Activity—Word Search

The words listed below are important terms relating to bailments. The words read forward, backward, up, down, and diagonally, but always in a straight line and never skipping letters. Circle each word you find. *SCORE*

P	L	Q	O	L	L	A	O	T	S	G	U	E	S	T
R	I	V	L	D	D	G	N	I	U	B	E	Q	N	Z
I	A	L	M	O	C	E	X	B	D	A	O	E	M	T
V	Q	M	N	B	O	M	P	M	D	I	M	I	B	L
A	I	O	O	F	M	O	N	E	I	L	C	S	I	R
T	I	P	O	D	M	C	S	E	I	O	F	R	L	E
E	C	G	U	L	O	F	L	A	C	R	O	Z	L	P
C	P	B	M	C	N	T	B	N	M	F	L	L	O	E
A	A	A	H	P	C	L	P	A	M	E	O	X	F	E
R	E	I	R	R	A	C	R	K	T	E	F	H	L	K
R	G	L	L	I	R	D	O	G	F	O	T	C	A	L
I	G	E	C	N	R	H	J	S	T	M	B	I	D	E
E	L	E	O	V	I	B	T	X	H	R	I	C	I	T
R	P	L	L	N	E	Z	Q	T	D	O	M	P	N	O
S	S	G	L	L	R	T	A	Y	M	O	L	N	G	H

act of God
bailee
bailor
bill of lading
carrier
common carrier
guest
hotelkeeper
lien
private carrier
special bailment

______

UNIT 5 BAILMENTS

Review

NAME________________________ DATE__________

SCORE__________

Review

PART 1: Indicate whether the following statements are true or false by circling either "true" or "false" in the Answers column.

	ANSWERS		SCORE
1. If a bailment has no specific time limit, it cannot be terminated by either party.	true	false	1.______
2. A bailment may involve real property such as land.	true	false	2.______
3. An illegal transaction cannot be the subject of a bailment.	true	false	3.______
4. The bailor does not have to be the owner of the property being bailed.	true	false	4.______
5. The standard of care required in a bailment depends on the amount of the consideration paid for the bailment.	true	false	5.______
6. A bailee may be held liable to a bailor for failing to observe the terms of the bailment.	true	false	6.______
7. A lease of a car for a two-year period would be considered a bailment.	true	false	7.______
8. Parties to a bailment may agree to limit the liability of the bailee.	true	false	8.______
9. A hotel has a greater responsibility toward a hotel guest than it does toward a business guest.	true	false	9.______
10. A bill of lading is given by the consignor to the consignee.	true	false	10.______

PART 2: For each statement, write the letter of the best answer in the Answers column.

	ANSWERS	SCORE
1. Renting a public locker is not considered to be a bailment because (A) it does not involve personal property, (B) the owner of the locker never actually accepts delivery of the articles in the locker, (C) no consideration is given, (D) the agreement is not in writing.	________	1.______
2. The subject of a bailment may be (A) 20 shares of corporate stock, (B) a sailboat, (C) a sweater, (D) all of these answers.	________	2.______
3. For a bailment to exist there must be (A) a transfer of possession, (B) a transfer of title, (C) a written lease, (D) real property of any type.	________	3.______
4. In a gratuitous bailment, (A) both parties benefit, (B) only the bailor or the bailee benefits, (C) no one benefits, (D) only a third party benefits.	________	4.______
5. The relationship between a bank and one of its depositors is that of (A) bailor-bailee, (B) trustor-trustee, (C) debtor-creditor, (D) none of these answers.	________	5.______
6. Grimm picked up a wallet that had been left on a bus. This is an example of (A) an express bailment, (B) a constructive bailment, (C) a bailment implied in fact, (D) a mutual benefit bailment.	________	6.______
7. Curtis wanted to borrow money from a bank. The bank wanted collateral for the loan, so Curtis deposited some of her stock with the bank as security. This is an example of a (A) consignment, (B) pawn, (C) pledge, (D) bailee's lien.	________	7.______
8. The standard of care required in a bailment for the sole benefit of the bailor is that of (A) minimal care, (B) extraordinary care, (C) slight care, (D) ordinary care.	________	8.______
9. Renting an item is an example of (A) a mutual benefit bailment, (B) a bailment by necessity, (C) a constructive bailment, (D) a bailment implied in fact.	________	9.______
10. A bailee's right to keep bailed property as security until paid for the work performed is known as the (A) bailee's mortgage, (B) bailee's lien, (C) consignment right, (D) pledge.	________	10.______

PART 3: Read the information below and answer the questions that follow. Write the letter of the best answer in the Answers column. *ANSWERS* *SCORE*

Bell, an onion farmer, shipped 400 sacks of onions from Jones, Long Island, to the Farmer's Market, Detroit, Michigan. The onions were shipped via Long Island Railroad, terms FOB Jones, Long Island.

1. The Long Island Railroad, which accepted the onions from Bell, transports goods for anyone who requests its services. This railroad is therefore considered a (A) consignee, (B) consignor, (C) common carrier, (D) private carrier. ________ 1.______
2. The rates charged by the Long Island Railroad for shipping goods from Jones, Long Island, to Detroit, Michigan, are subject to the regulations of the (A) Federal Trade Commission, (B) Public Service Commission, (C) Interstate Commerce Commission, (D) Intrastate Commerce Commission. ________ 2.______
3. The onions were shipped according to the railroad's regular shipping conditions and without any unusual delay. When they reached their destination, however, onions in several of the bags had spoiled. The railroad is liable for (A) the value of the spoiled onions, (B) negligence in not speeding delivery to prevent spoilage, (C) negligence in accepting goods that were subject to spoiling, (D) no part of the loss, because of the nature of the goods. ________ 3.______
4. When the onions arrived in Detroit, the Farmer's Market was unable to unload them for two days. The carrier levied a charge for this delay. This charge is known as (A) demurrage, (B) fee simple, (C) a tariff, (D) a lien. ________ 4.______

PART 4: Read the case problem below and then answer the questions that follow. *SCORE*

Blake drove her car into a parking lot and turned the keys over to an attendant, who parked the car for her. There was a sign posted in the attendant's building that read "Not responsible for loss of or damage to cars in excess of $500." Blake never saw the sign. Two hours later, a tornado hit the parking lot and destroyed Blake's car, which was valued at $10,000. Blake seeks to collect $10,000 from the owner of the parking lot.

1. What is the legal relationship between Blake and the parking lot owner?

____ 1.______

2. Is Blake bound by the limitation of liability stated on the sign posted in the attendant's building? Explain your answer.

____

____ 2.______

3. Must the parking lot owner pay Blake for her loss? Explain your answer.

____

____ 3.______

4. If the parking lot owner is obligated to pay Blake, what amount would the owner have to pay? Why?

____

____ 4.______

UNIT 6 AGENCY AND EMPLOYMENT

Chapter 25 The Employer-Employee Relationship

NAME________________________________ DATE______________

SCORE______________

Study Guide and Review

PART 1: Indicate whether each statement below is true or false by circling "true" or "false" in the Answers column.

	ANSWERS		SCORE
1. An employment contract for more than onc year must be in writing.	true	false	1.______
2. An employee can be forced to join a union as a condition for being hired.	true	false	2.______
3. Employers have a legal right to tell employees what tasks are to be performed and how the tasks are to be performed.	true	false	3.______
4. The Fair Labor Standards Act requires certain employers to provide employees a legal minimum hourly wage, plus one and one-half times their regular hourly wage for all hours worked over 40 hours per week.	true	false	4.______
5. The Occupational Safety and Health Act requires employers to provide employees with safe working conditions in the buildings where they work.	true	false	5.______
6. An employer, as well as the employee, may be liable for torts committed by the employee who is acting within the scope of employment.	true	false	6.______
7. An employer may end a contract with an employee at any time without liability.	true	false	7.______
8. If the employment contract does not specify a length of employment, an employee may quit a job at any time.	true	false	8.______
9. An employer has no right to dismiss an employee who consistently fails to do the job.	true	false	9.______
10. Extreme negligence by an employee would prevent recovery under the workers' compensation laws of the various states that have these laws.	truc	false	10.______

PART 2: In each of the following case problems, give a decision by writing "yes" or "no" in the space provided. Then, in sentence form, give a reason for your decision.

SCORE

1. The Disco Roller Skating Rink advertised in a local newspaper for a male floor guard. Schantz, a female, applied for the job and was turned down by the rink manager, who claimed that she could not handle the job because it was for "tough males." Could Schantz legally be turned down for this reason?

Decision: ____

Reason: ____

____ 1.______

2. Steeper was hired under a three-year contract to be head accountant for the Alliance Tool Company. When the owner discovered that Steeper was giving a competing tool company confidential information about Alliance, he fired Steeper. Steeper sued for breach of contract, claiming that since his contract had not expired, he could not be fired. Was Steeper correct?

Decision: ____

Reason: ____

____ 2.______

SCORE

3. Tydings Garage was required by state law to provide ventilating equipment to protect its workers. Because this equipment was not installed, one mechanic suffered carbon monoxide poisoning and was unable to work for several weeks. Is the mechanic entitled to benefits under the Workers' Compensation Act?

Decision: ______________________________

Reason: ______________________________

______________________________ 3. ______

4. Baxter was employed by Veterans Motors as a mechanic. He worked from 8 a.m. to 5 p.m., with an hour for lunch. After many warnings, Baxter continued to take much more than an hour for lunch. Would Veterans Motors be justified in discharging Baxter?

Decision: ______________________________

Reason: ______________________________

______________________________ 4. ______

5. Marston worked in a supermarket packing groceries and carrying the bags to the customers' cars. While carrying some groceries one day, he carelessly dropped a heavy bag on a customer's foot. Is the supermarket owner liable to the customer for the injuries caused by this accident?

Decision: ______________________________

Reason: ______________________________

______________________________ 5. ______

PART 3: Read the information given below, then answer the questions that follow. Write the letter of the best answer in the Answers column.

ANSWERS SCORE

Curran was employed by Bond Wholesale Foods to deliver food supplied to grocery stores.

1. Curran is legally known as (A) an assignee, (B) an employee, (C) a merchant, (D) an employer. ______ 1. ______
2. After Curran had been employed for some time, he tried to organize his fellow workers into a union. Curran is allowed to organize his fellow workers, without interference from Bond Wholesale Foods, under the provisions of the (A) National Labor Relations Act, (B) Federal Fair Labor Standards Act, (C) Wage and Hour Law, (D) Occupational Safety and Health Act. ______ 2. ______
3. As a result of Curran's efforts, the workers formed a union that was recognized by Bond Wholesale Foods. Curran, as union representative, negotiated a contract with higher wages and improved working conditions. Since both the employees and the company approved the contract, it is known as (A) a workers' agreement, (B) a collective bargaining agreement, (C) an equal pay agreement, (D) a workers' compensation agreement. ______ 3. ______
4. Curran, while making a delivery, fell and broke his leg. As a result, he could not work for several weeks. Curran's medical bills, as well as a weekly income while he could not work, would be paid under the (A) Unemployment Insurance Law, (B) Fair Labor Standards Act, (C) Occupational Safety and Health Act, (D) state workers' compensation laws. ______ 4. ______
5. Bond Wholesale Foods prohibits its employees from conducting anything other than company business during working hours. Curran ran a part-time storm window business on the side. While making deliveries for Bond, he often met with customers for his storm window business. If Bonds discovers what Curran is doing, it could (A) report Curran to the affirmative action office, (B) report Curran to OSHA, (C) fire Curran, (D) have Curran arrested. ______ 5. ______

UNIT 6 AGENCY AND EMPLOYMENT

Chapter 26 The Principal-Agent Relationship

NAME________________________ DATE__________

SCORE__________

Study Guide and Review

PART 1: Indicate whether each statement below is true or false by circling "true" or "false" in the Answers column.

	ANSWERS	*SCORE*
1. An agent is a person who transacts business with third parties in place of and at the request of the principal.	true false	1.______
2. In carrying out their duties, agents do not have the right to make independent decisions or to exercise judgment.	true false	2.______
3. A person may act both as an employee and as an agent.	true false	3.______
4. Agents who do not receive compensation are called gratuitous agents.	true false	4.______
5. A principal-agent relationship may be created in an emergency situation.	true false	5.______
6. A special agent has the authority to perform acts that relate to all business matters of the principal.	true false	6.______
7. All profits that result from the agency belong to the principal.	true false	7.______
8. A principal may legally appoint an agent only by means of a written contract.	true false	8.______
9. An independent contractor is an agent.	true false	9.______
10. A real estate agent hired to sell a house is considered a special agent.	true false	10.______

PART 2: For each situation below, indicate the way in which the agency relationship was created by writing the correct letter in the Answers column.

(A) agency created by contract

(B) agency created by appearance

(C) agency created by ratification

(D) agency created by necessity

	ANSWERS	*SCORE*
1. Arlis left Marvin, a friend, at her (Arlis's) fruit and vegetable stand with instructions only to tell customers that the stand would open two hours late because of an emergency. While Arlis was gone, Marvin sold fruit and vegetables to several customers.	________	1.______
2. Calkins used Green's car to drive Green's parents to a family reunion 50 miles away. The car developed engine trouble, and Calkins had to have it repaired in order to reach the destination. Calkins presented the repair bill to Green.	________	2.______
3. Beaty signed a three-year written contract to manage Richard's Tour Guide Agency in New York City.	________	3.______
4. Downs asked Erlman to purchase a stereo and charge it to her (Downs's) account with her credit card. Downs asked Erlman to pay no more than $750. Instead, Erlman charged a stereo costing $1,000. When the bill arrived, Downs paid the $1,000.	________	4.______
5. Count is employed under a five-year contract as a sales representative for Arnold's Clothes Unlimited. Count sold merchandise on credit to Barnes's Department Store, which must pay the bill in 30 days.	________	5.______

PART 3: In each of the following case problems, give a decision by writing "yes" or "no" in the space provided. Then, in sentence form, give a reason for your decision.

SCORE

1. Todd was a salesperson for the Marcum Textbook Company. The company provided her with a car to travel to various high schools within a specific territory in Wyoming. While she was driving within the speed limit on a highway, her company car was struck by a hit-and-run driver, causing $200 in damages. Todd paid for the repairs out of her own pocket, but the Marcum Company refused to repay Todd, claiming it had no legal obligation to do so. Was the Marcum Company correct?

Decision: ____________________

Reason: ____________________

____________________ 1. ______

2. O'Brien, a retiree, decided to invest in a fast-growing company that was selling its stock for $20 per share. He appointed Walford, a person with a good business background, as his agent to buy 50 shares of Xeon stock. Unknown to O'Brien, Walford had already purchased 100 shares of Xeon stock for himself when it was being offered at $10 per share. Walford then sold 50 of his shares to O'Brien for $20 per share and kept the profit for himself. When O'Brien found this out, he demanded that Walford take the stock back, stating that what Walford did was a breach of trust. Must Walford comply?

Decision: ____________________

Reason: ____________________

____________________ 2. ______

3. DiFabio, an adult, hired Nichols, a minor, as general manager of a service station and authorized him to buy supplies. Nichols contracted to buy some supplies that were not needed. DiFabio claimed that the contract was not valid because Nichols was a minor and therefore could not act as an agent. Is DiFabio legally correct in claiming that he is not bound by Nichols's contract?

Decision: ____________________

Reason: ____________________

____________________ 3. ______

4. As purchasing agent for the Delton Company, Millson often bought materials from the Howard Supply Company. After he was discharged by the Delton Company, Millson bought something for himself from Howard Supply but charged it to Delton. Howard Supply knew nothing about Millson's dismissal. Can Howard Supply hold the Delton Company liable for Millson's purchase?

Decision: ____________________

Reason: ____________________

____

____

____________________ 4. ______

NAME ______________________ DATE ____________

5. Fox, who was going in the Army, contracted with Scutti Auto Sales to sell his car for a commission. Scutti Auto Sales advanced $500 to Fox, with the understanding that the $500 would be paid back out of the proceeds from the sale. Three weeks later, before the car was sold, Fox changed his mind and tried to terminate the agency. Can Fox legally terminate the agency? *SCORE*

Decision: ______________________

Reason: ______________________

____

____

______________________ 5. ______

PART 4: In each of the following situations, the underlined party is liable for violating a specific principal or agent obligation. In the space provided, identify the obligation that has been violated.

	ANSWERS	*SCORE*
1. Conte collected credit payments from Nill's dry cleaning customers. Because he put the money from the collections in his regular bank account, he could not determine the correct amount to send to Nill.	______	1. ______
2. Mendon sent Roberts, one of his traveling salespersons, to investigate sales possibilities in a distant city. Mendon later refused to pay Roberts for his trip expenses.	______	2. ______
3. Baskin told Robbins, his salesperson, to sell door-to-door in a neighboring town. While carrying out his work, Robbins was arrested and fined for not having a license required by town ordinance. Baskin refused to pay Robbins the amount of the fine.	______	3. ______
4. Burley agreed to sell Arno's boat for a commission. Burley had previously been hired to purchase a boat for Fisher. Without disclosing either agreement, Burley bought Arno's boat, sold it to Fisher, and tried to collect a commission from both.	______	4. ______
5. Thayer, a sales clerk for Quarrels Card Shop, was told to place a certain brand of greeting card on sale. Thayer placed all of the greeting cards in the shop on sale, resulting in a considerable loss to Quarrels.	______	5. ______

PART 5: For each statement, write the letter of the best answer in the Answers column.

	ANSWERS	*SCORE*
1. When an agent makes a contract for a deceased principal, the contract is (A) binding on the agent, (B) binding on the principal's estate, (C) voidable, (D) void.	______	1. ______
2. Doan authorized Marple to sell Doan's car for not less than $2,000 for a commission of 10%. Marple sold the car for $2,400. How much must Marple give Doan? (A) $2,000, (B) $2,000 less commission, (C) $2,200, (D) $2,400 less commission.	______	2. ______
3. An agent is given formal written authority to sign checks for her principal. This formal written authorization is known as (A) an affidavit, (B) a power of attorney, (C) a notary, (D) a certification.	______	3. ______

ANSWERS SCORE

4. Morales, general agent for the Kincaid Manufacturing Company, was notified of the company's bankruptcy. Which statement regarding the principal-agent relationship is correct: (A) contracts made by the agent after bankruptcy of the principal are binding on the principal, (B) a general agent is liable as a guarantor of the bankrupt principal's unpaid accounts, (C) the principal's bankruptcy has no effect on the principal-agent agreement, (D) bankruptcy of the principal terminates the agency agreement. ________ 4.______
5. A principal-agent relationship may be terminated by (A) death of the third party, (B) request of the third party, (C) mutual agreement between principal and agent, (D) bankruptcy of the third party. ________ 5.______

Activity—Finding the Facts

Read the following paragraph. Then, in the space provided, answer the questions below. SCORE

Vonnie Everard owned several apartment buildings in Providence, Rhode Island. Since she planned to take a European trip during June, she composed and signed a power of attorney designating Carmen Longo, also of Providence, as her agent. The power of attorney read, in part, as follows: "I, Vonnie Everard, hereby appoint Carmen Longo to collect rent from tenants in all my apartment buildings, and to pay all bills connected with these apartments by signing and executing checks as my agent." A special checking account, on which checks were to be written, was set up at the Lincoln Alliance Bank in Providence. Longo was directed to place all rent money collected in the special account.

1. Is every agency created by means of a power of attorney such as the one in the example above?

____ 1.______

2. Is Longo classified as a general or a special agent? ________________ 2.______

3. Could the authority given to Longo have been given orally? ________________ 3.______

4. According to the power of attorney, does Longo have the authority to authorize repairs to any of the apartments?

____ 4.______

5. Longo did not follow Everard's instructions for paying bills. As a result, Everard had to pay a late charge to many companies. Can Everard collect from Longo the amount of any service charge paid?

____ 5.______

UNIT 6 AGENCY AND EMPLOYMENT

Chapter 27 Responsibility of Principal and Agent to Third Parties

NAME________________________________ DATE__________

SCORE__________

Study Guide and Review

PART 1: Indicate whether each statement below is true or false by circling "true" or "false" in the Answers column.

	ANSWERS		SCORE
1. An agent's implied authority is the authority understood as necessary to carry out the purpose of the agency.	true	false	1.______
2. If a tort occurs while an agent is pursuing her or his own interests, the principal can still be held liable.	true	false	2.______
3. A principal whose identity is not known to the third party is a disclosed principal.	true	false	3.______
4. A power of attorney is an example of express authority in a principal-agent relationship.	true	false	4.______
5. An agent acting within the scope of agency cannot be held liable for torts committed against a third party.	true	false	5.______
6. Principals may ratify contracts made by unauthorized agents.	true	false	6.______
7. An agent has the apparent authority to perform those duties not expressly given by the principal.	true	false	7.______
8. If a third party learns that a contract he or she made with an agent was actually made for an undisclosed principal, the third party can then enforce the contract against either the principal or the agent.	true	false	8.______
9. The law does not recognize the agent as a party to the contract when he or she acts within the scope of authority.	true	false	9.______
10. When dealing with third parties, an agent is personally liable if he or she does not disclose the principal's identity.	true	false	10.______

PART 2: For each statement, write the letter of the best answer in the Answers column.

	ANSWERS	SCORE
1. Frost was hired as general manager of Casey's snow plowing business. As general manager, Frost has (A) implied authority to hire and fire people to help clear snow, (B) implied authority to sell the snow plowing business, (C) implied authority to purchase new equipment, (D) actual authority to cancel equipment orders placed by Casey.	________	1.______
2. A principal is generally not liable for her or his agent's (A) torts, (B) contracts, (C) criminal acts, (D) false statements.	________	2.______
3. A principal whose identity is not known to the third party with whom the agent makes a contract is called (A) an independent contractor, (B) a fiduciary, (C) an undisclosed principal, (D) an irrevocable principal.	________	3.______
4. Apparent authority is (A) express authority, (B) implied authority, (C) the extent of the agent's authority, (D) authority that a principal leads third parties to believe that the agent has.	________	4.______
5. When a principal approves of an agent's unauthorized act, the principal has (A) ratified the act, (B) rejected the act, (C) elected to either ratify or reject the act, (D) acted in the scope of authority.	________	5.______
6. A principal is generally bound by contracts an agent makes with third parties on behalf of the principal if the agent acts (A) quickly, (B) within the scope of authority, (C) to the principal's advantage, (D) on commission.	________	6.______

ANSWERS SCORE

7. When a third party discovers the identity of an undisclosed principal, the third party (A) may hold both the principal and the agent liable on the contract, (B) may hold only the principal liable on the contract, (C) may hold only the agent liable, (D) may hold either the principal or the agent liable, but not both. ________ 7. ______
8. If the agent does not include the principal's name on a written contract, (A) both principal and agent are bound by the contract, (B) only the agent is bound, (C) only the principal is bound, (D) the contract is not binding. ________ 8. ______
9. A person who pretends to be an agent (A) is personally liable to a third party, (B) binds the principal, (C) binds the third party, (D) has the power of ratification. ________ 9. ______
10. The proper signature by an agent, R. M. Figs, on behalf of a principal, Normen Corner, is (A) R. M. Figs, (B) Normen Corner by R. M. Figs, Agent, (C) R. M. Figs, Agent, (D) Normen Corner, Principal. ________ 10. ______

PART 3: For each of the following case problems, give a decision by writing "yes" or "no" in the space provided. Then, in sentence form, give a reason for your answer.

SCORE

1. While she was away on a business trip, Martin, a storeowner, left Maxim, one of her salesclerks, in charge of her store. During this time, a heavy rainstorm flooded the basement. Maxim hired two men to remove some merchandise from the basement to save it from water damage. Is Martin legally obligated to pay the two men?

Decision: ________________________________

Reason: ________________________________

____

________________________________ 1. ______

2. Lerner, a sales agent for Burke, sold jewelry to Polk, stating that it was platinum. Later, when Polk learned that the jewelry was white gold, he sued Burke. Burke claimed that he was not liable, since he had not authorized Lerner to make such a statement about the jewelry. Is Burke liable for damages?

Decision: ________________________________

Reason: ________________________________

________________________________ 2. ______

3. Hammer was employed as a salesperson by the Outgoing Merchandise Company. In the company's name, with a view to boosting sales, she entered into a contract with a TV station for a series of spot announcements. The Outgoing Company refused to pay for the advertising, claiming that Hammer did not have authorization. Is the Outgoing Company liable to the TV station?

Decision: ________________________________

Reason: ________________________________

____

____

________________________________ 3. ______

UNIT 6 AGENCY AND EMPLOYMENT

Review

NAME____ DATE____________

SCORE____________

Review

PART 1: Indicate whether each statement below is true or false by circling "true" or "false" in the Answers column.

	ANSWERS		*SCORE*
1. One obligation of an agent to a principal is indemnification.	true	false	1.______
2. Implied authority is a type of actual authority.	true	false	2.______
3. If the principal terminates the agent's actual authority, the agent's apparent authority is automatically terminated as well.	true	false	3.______
4. If an agent refuses to continue to work for the principal, the principal-agent relationship is automatically terminated.	true	false	4.______
5. A person may be an employee and also act as an agent for the employer.	true	false	5.______
6. A principal-agent relationship is created only through an oral or written contract.	true	false	6.______
7. Under the Occupational Safety and Health Act, employers must provide employees with safe working conditions.	true	false	7.______
8. Employees who are covered by workers' compensation laws are entitled to certain benefits if they are injured on the job, regardless of whether the employee was at fault.	truc	false	8.______
9. A person can act as an agent for both parties to a transaction even if neither party is aware of the agent's dual status.	true	false	9.______
10. An agent who makes a secret profit is entitled to keep the money even if the principal discovers it and demands its return.	true	false	10.______

PART 2: Based on the information given below, write the letter of the best answer in the Answers column for each statement.

Whitmore, a used-car dealer, hired Chambers as a sales representative for six months at a weekly salary of $200, plus commission.

	ANSWERS	*SCORE*
1. Chambers paid for some repairs that were required when she was demonstrating a car to a customer. Her right to collect this amount from Whitmore is called the right of (A) accounting, (B) compensation, (C) indemnification, (D) reimbursement.	________	1.______
2. If, after Chambers had sold several used cars, Whitmore found that she was a minor, (A) her contracts would still be valid, (B) her contracts would be voidable, (C) her contracts would be invalid, (D) she could not legally make any more contracts.	________	2.______
3. After a customer purchased a used car on the basis of Chambers's remark that the car was "a bargain at $1,500," the customer found that the engine was in very bad condition. The customer may hold Whitmore legally liable for (A) fraud, (B) undue influence, (C) deceit, (D) nothing.	________	3.______
4. Chambers can be referred to as (A) a general agent, (B) a special agent, (C) an implied agent, (D) a public agent.	________	4.______
5. If a customer is injured in an accident caused solely by Chambers's careless driving, that customer can sue Whitmore because (A) the principal has a duty to live up to the terms of the contract, (B) the principal is bound by any knowledge acquired by the agent, (C) the principal is liable for torts of an agent acting within the scope of the agency, (D) the principal has a duty to compensate the agent for any loss or damage.	________	5.______

PART 3: For each of the following case problems, give a decision by writing "yes" or "no" in the space provided. Then, in sentence form, give a reason for your decision.

SCORE

1. Bauman agreed to act as general manager of the Furniture Mart for three years. Is it necessary for this agreement to be in writing?

Decision: ______________________________

Reason: ______________________________

______________________________ 1. ______

2. Frances worked as a cook in the Little Chef Restaurant. Melanson, owner of the restaurant, had not anticipated the large Thanksgiving Day business, and so authorized Frances to buy several food items at a local food market where Melanson often did business. Was Frances a special agent?

Decision: ______________________________

Reason: ______________________________

______________________________ 2. ______

3. Drake, owner of Rent-A-Car, hired Pincus to purchase five new cars for the business. On the day that Pincus made the purchase, Drake, who was on vacation, died in a hotel fire. Was the contract made by Pincus valid?

Decision: ______________________________

Reason: ______________________________

______________________________ 3. ______

4. Pitnell authorized her office manager to employ an additional bookkeeper. The office manager hired a bookkeeper and a clerk typist. Pitnell refused to pay the clerk typist's salary, claiming that because the office manager had exceeded her authority, she (Pitnell) was not liable. Is Pitnell correct?

Decision: ______________________________

Reason: ______________________________

______________________________ 4. ______

5. Jackson hired Ames, a minor, to manage a store. Without Jackson's knowledge, Ames bought merchandise for the store from the Rustic Supply Company. Jackson later refused to pay for the merchandise on the grounds that he was not bound by a minor's contract. Is Jackson bound by this contract?

Decision: ______________________________

Reason: ______________________________

______________________________ 5. ______

UNIT 7 COMMERCIAL PAPER

Chapter 28 The Nature of Commercial Paper

NAME________________________________ DATE____________

SCORE____________

Study Guide and Review

PART 1: For each statement, write the letter of the best answer in the Answers column.

	ANSWERS	SCORE
1. A check is issued by the (A) maker, (B) payee, (C) drawee, (D) drawer.	______	1.______
2. A promissory note must contain (A) words indicating a promise to pay, (B) the words IOU, (C) a certificate of deposit, (D) a date.	______	2.______
3. The signature on a negotiable instrument must (A) be printed or stamped on the instrument, (B) be that of the maker or drawer, (C) appear in the body of the instrument, (D) appear in the lower right-hand corner.	______	3.______
4. A written order by one person on a second person to pay a third person is a (A) promissory note, (B) certificate of deposit, (C) draft, (D) receipt.	______	4.______
5. The omission of the word "order" or "bearer" on a promissory note renders it (A) voidable, (B) void, (C) negotiable, (D) nonnegotiable.	______	5.______
6. The term "nonnegotiable" means (A) void, (B) not cash, (C) not readily transferable from one person to another, (D) not payable.	______	6.______
7. An instrument is payable on demand or at a definite time if it is payable (A) at someone's death, (B) upon the happening of a certain condition, (C) on, before, or after a specified date, (D) at a bank.	______	7.______
8. A check that contains the words "Three hundred fifty dollars" and the figures "$3.50" is (A) payable in the amount of $350, (B) illegal, (C) payable in the amount of $3.50, (D) void.	______	8.______
9. An instrument is not payable in a sum certain in money and thus is not negotiable if (A) it is payable in foreign currency adopted as the legal currency of that foreign country, (B) it is payable with interest, (C) the amount in figures is omitted, (D) the person required to pay the instrument has the option to pay something in addition to money.	______	9.______
10. A check is (A) a written promise, (B) usually payable at a certain time, (C) payable immediately, (D) not a substitute for cash.	______	10.______
11. Which of the following contains the necessary words of negotiability: (A) pay to Mary Roe, (B) please pay Mary Roe, (C) pay to holder, Mary Roe, (D) pay to the order of Mary Roe.	______	11.______
12. Brown signed a document unconditionally promising to pay a certain sum of money on a definite day to the order of Nevarez. Nevarez is known as the (A) maker, (B) payee, (C) drawer, (D) drawee.	______	12.______
13. A promissory note is not negotiable if it is (A) not dated, (B) payable 30 days after the death of the maker, (C) signed by two people, (D) payable 30 days after the date of the promissory note.	______	13.______
14. A note or check payable in a foreign currency that is the legal currency of that foreign country is (A) nonnegotiable, (B) fully negotiable, (C) not payable in the dollar equivalent of that currency, (D) void.	______	14.______
15. If the date of issue is omitted from a note or check, its negotiability is (A) restricted, (B) voided, (C) not affected, (D) postponed.	______	15.______

PART 2: Indicate in the Answers column whether each of the following is a negotiable (N) or nonnegotiable (NN) instrument. (Assume that all other requirements of negotiable instruments not specifically mentioned are present.)

	ANSWERS	*SCORE*
1. An unsigned check.	______	1. ______
2. A note on which the person who made out the instrument signed with an "X."	______	2. ______
3. An instrument made payable to "Bearer."	______	3. ______
4. A promissory note payable 10 days before February 8, 1988.	______	4. ______
5. A check that is not dated.	______	5. ______
6. An oral promise to pay one thousand dollars.	______	6. ______
7. A check on which the name of the payee is omitted.	______	7. ______
8. A signed promissory note containing the words "I promise to pay 500 pounds of scrap iron to the order of Merle Thomas."	______	8. ______
9. A draft payable "at sight."	______	9. ______
10. A draft in which the drawee's name has been omitted.	______	10. ______

PART 3: Indicate whether each statement below is true or false by circling either "true" or "false" in the Answers column.

	ANSWERS		*SCORE*
1. A person to whom a negotiable instrument is transferred obtains special privileges.	true	false	1. ______
2. A check is an instrument that is payable on demand.	true	false	2. ______
3. The drawee of a check is always a bank.	true	false	3. ______
4. An instrument that places conditions on the promise or order to pay is negotiable.	true	false	4. ______
5. A negotiable instrument that is a written promise to pay money is a draft.	true	false	5. ______
6. The party who promises to pay a promissory note is called the drawee.	true	false	6. ______
7. A promissory note need not be in writing.	true	false	7. ______
8. A promissory note is an order to pay.	true	false	8. ______
9. An instrument made payable to "Myself" is considered payable to bearer.	true	false	9. ______
10. An instrument that is payable "15 days after I paint my house" is negotiable.	true	false	10. ______

Activity—Crossword Puzzle

Across

2. Party making payment, generally a bank.
3. Substitute for money.
7. Written promise to pay.
8. Transferable.
10. Legal currency.
11. Promise by a bank to repay a depositor.

Down

1. Type of draft.
2. Order by one party to a second party to pay a third party.
4. The person who issues a check.
5. The person ordering payment.
6. Payable to anyone who has possession.
7. Party to receive payment.
9. Payable to a named party.

UNIT 7 COMMERCIAL PAPER

Chapter 29 The Negotiation and Discharge of Commercial Paper

NAME____________________ DATE__________

SCORE__________

Study Guide and Review

PART 1: Indicate whether each statement below is true or false by circling either "true" or "false" in the Answers column.

	ANSWERS		SCORE
1. A payee of commercial paper may transfer that instrument to someone by negotiation.	true	false	1.____
2. The indorsement that limits the liability ordinarily undertaken by an indorser is known as a restrictive indorsement.	true	false	2.____
3. An indorsement that states the name of the person to whom the instrument is being transferred is a special indorsement.	true	false	3.____
4. A check payable to "cash" must be negotiated by indorsement and delivery.	true	false	4.____
5. The purpose of an indorsement is to transfer ownership of commercial paper.	true	false	5.____
6. An accommodation indorsement is often used to help someone who does not have good credit.	true	false	6.____
7. A person who has a negotiable instrument containing a blank indorsement can legally change this indorsement into a special indorsement.	true	false	7.____
8. A blank indorsement makes the instrument payable to the bearer.	true	false	8.____
9. The use of a qualified indorsement makes an instrument nonnegotiable.	true	false	9.____
10. Marking a promissory note "void" is one way of canceling the instrument.	true	false	10.____
11. "For deposit only" is a special indorsement.	true	false	11.____
12. An instrument with a blank indorsement may be transferred from one person to another by delivery alone, without further indorsement.	true	false	12.____
13. Bearer paper may be negotiated by voluntary delivery alone.	true	false	13.____
14. An instrument with a blank indorsement should not be mailed because if the instrument is lost, anyone could collect without proving ownership of the instrument.	true	false	14.____
15. A special indorsement must contain the words "order" or "bearer."	true	false	15.____

PART 2: For each statement, write the letter of the best answer in the Answers column.

	ANSWERS	SCORE
1. Barbara Allen indorses her paycheck "For deposit only—Barbara Allen." This indorsement is (A) blank, (B) restrictive, (C) special, (D) qualified.	______	1.____
2. The following indorsement by Walter Bly, the payee of a check, makes the check payable to bearer: (A) Walter Bly, (B) Pay to the order of Herb Winthrop, (signed) Walter Bly, (C) Pay to Herb Winthrop, (signed) Walter Bly, (D) Pay to Herb Winthrop or Order, (signed) Walter Bly.	______	2.____
3. Varden wanted to make a bank deposit by mail. The safest indorsement for her to use on checks deposited this way is (A) a special indorsement, (B) a blank indorsement, (C) an accommodation indorsement, (D) a restrictive indorsement.	______	3.____
4. Barron negotiated a check that she received from Cleary by making the following indorsement: "Pay to the order of Blythe Love—Jane Barron." Love may now legally negotiate this check by (A) delivery only, (B) indorsement only, (C) either indorsement or delivery, (D) both indorsement and delivery.	______	4.____
5. To be valid, an indorsement (A) must be typed, (B) must be handwritten, (C) may be either typed or handwritten, (D) must be printed.	______	5.____

PART 3: In each of the following case problems, give a decision by writing "yes" or "no" in the space provided. Then, in sentence form, give a reason for your decision. SCORE

1. Falvo made out a check payable to cash and gave the check to Gamber. Gamber left this check on his desk while he attended a meeting. When Gamber returned, he discovered that the check had been stolen. Did the thief receive the check by negotiation?

   Decision: ______________________________

   Reason: ______________________________

   ______________________________ 1. ______

2. Freeman's house was burglarized, and several checks were stolen, one of which was made out to cash. The thief who stole the check passed it on to another party. Did the transfer by the thief to another party constitute a negotiation of the check?

   Decision: ______________________________

   Reason: ______________________________

   ______________________________ 2. ______

Activity—Indorsing Checks

Follow the directions given for each activity below. SCORE

1. James Tuttle wrote a check drawn on the Friendly Trust Bank, payable to Rachel Fellows in the amount of $500. Fellows owed $500 to Timothy Blanchard, so she indorsed the check and gave it to Blanchard.

   a. Who is the drawer? ______________________________ a. ______

   b. Who is the drawee? ______________________________ b. ______

   c. Who is the payee? ______________________________ c. ______

   d. Who is the indorser? ______________________________ d. ______

   e. Who is the indorsee? ______________________________ e. ______

2. Name each of the indorsements in the illustrations below.

a.
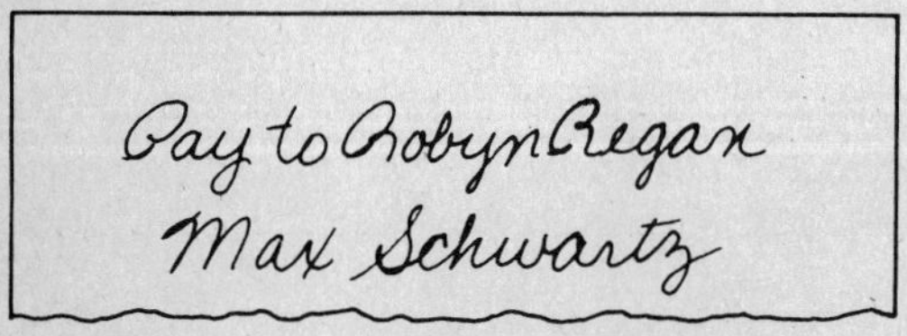

______________________________ a. ______

b.
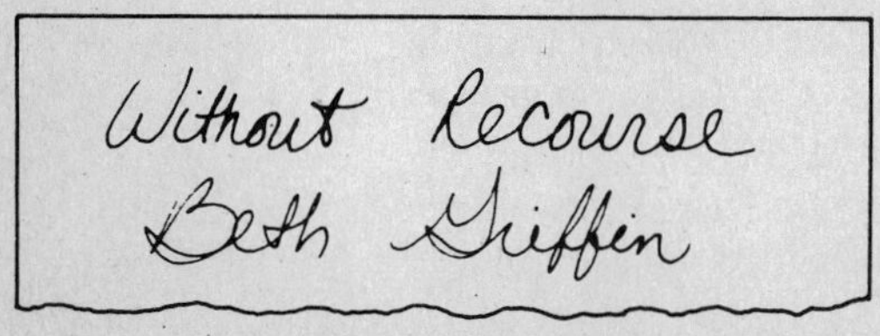

______________________________ b. ______

c.
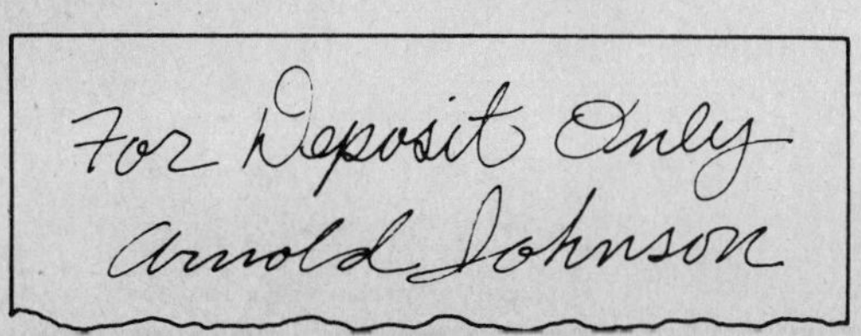

______________________________ c. ______

UNIT 7 COMMERCIAL PAPER

Chapter 30 Rights and Duties of Parties to Commercial Paper

NAME________________________ DATE____________

SCORE____________

Study Guide and Review

PART 1: Indicate whether each statement below is true or false by circling either "true" or "false" in the Answers column.

	ANSWERS		*SCORE*
1. Under the UCC, the holder of a check has 30 days after the date of issue to present it for payment or the drawer will not be liable.	true	false	1.______
2. If presentment of a promissory note is late, the maker is discharged from any liability.	true	false	2.______
3. A person whose name is forged to an instrument has a personal defense against all holders.	true	false	3.______
4. A promissory note falls due on January 8. Proper presentment may be made on January 9.	true	false	4.______
5. Kuhn, the payee of a promissory note, changed the amount due from \$60 to \$600. The maker can be held liable for \$600.	true	false	5.______
6. Nonnegotiable instruments are subject to the rules of ordinary contracts and may be transferred by assignment.	true	false	6.______

PART 2: For each of the following case problems, give a decision by writing "yes" or "no" in the space provided. Then, in sentence form, give a reason for your decision.

SCORE

1. Blair wanted to make a gift to his son Eric but did not have enough cash on hand. Instead, he gave Eric a \$5,000 promissory note, payable in 30 days. Eric negotiated the note ten days later to his friend Tom. When Tom tried to collect on the note from Blair, Blair refused to pay, claiming that there was no consideration for the execution of the note. Is this a valid defense against payment to Tom?

Decision: ____

Reason: ____

____ 1.______

2. Curran bought a new car from Superior Motors. He paid \$1,000 in cash and gave a promissory note for the balance of the purchase price. Superior negotiated the note to Calumet Bank and received cash in return. Curran then found the car's transmission was defective, and he refused to make any payments to Calumet Bank. If it had no knowledge of the defective transmission, is Calumet Bank considered a holder in due course?

Decision: ____

Reason: ____

____

____ 2.______

PART 3: In the Answers column at the right, write the letter of the word or words in Column 1 that best match each statement in Column 2.

COLUMN 1

(A) secondary party
(B) real defenses
(C) primary party
(D) notice of dishonor
(E) presentment
(F) improper presentment
(G) unauthorized completion
(H) ordinary holder
(I) holder in due course concept
(J) accommodation parties who sign as indorsers

COLUMN 2	*ANSWERS*	*SCORE*
1. May be given orally or in writing.	______	1. ______
2. Cannot be used against ultimate consumers.	______	2. ______
3. Discharges liability of secondary parties.	______	3. ______
4. Parties having secondary liability.	______	4. ______
5. A personal defense.	______	5. ______
6. Good against all holders, including a holder in due course.	______	6. ______
7. A demand for payment made by a holder of commercial paper.	______	7. ______
8. Has unconditional liability for payment of commercial paper.	______	8. ______
9. Has conditional liability for payment of commercial paper.	______	9. ______
10. A person who does not qualify as a holder in due course.	______	10. ______

Activity—Analyzing Commercial Paper

The following promissory note was given to Erica Karvelos by Maria Schmidt as evidence of a $350 loan made by Karvelos to Schmidt. Karvelos indorsed this note and gave it to her niece as a wedding present. Study the note and then answer the questions that follow.

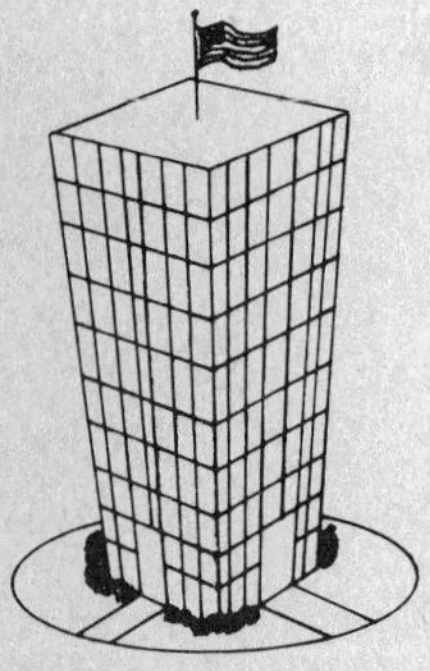

$ 350.00 June 25, 19--

Thirty days *after date* I *promise to pay*

to the order of Erica Karvelos

Three hundred fifty ------------------- *Dollars*

at The First National Bank of Boston, Boston, Massachusetts

Value received

No. ______ *Due* July 25, 19-- Maria A. Schmidt

SCORE

1. Who is primarily responsible for payment of this note? ______________________________ 1. ______

2. Is Erica Karvelos an ordinary holder or a holder in due course? ______________________________ 2. ______

3. Is the niece a holder or a holder in due course? ______________________________ 3. ______

4. What are the conditions that determine whether a person to whom commercial paper has been transferred is an ordinary holder or a holder in due course?
____
____
______________________________ 4. ______

UNIT 7 COMMERCIAL PAPER

Chapter 31 Checks and the Banking System

NAME____________________ DATE__________

SCORE__________

Study Guide and Review

PART 1: Indicate whether each statement below is true or false by circling either ''true'' or ''false'' in the Answers column.

	ANSWERS		*SCORE*
1. A stop-payment order may be telephoned to the bank.	true	false	1.______
2. When a depositor receives a monthly statement of bank transactions, that person has a duty to promptly advise the bank of any mistakes.	true	false	2.______
3. Writing a bad check is a criminal act that could lead to arrest of the drawer.	true	false	3.______
4. If the drawer's negligence contributes to the alteration of a check, loss resulting from the bank's payment of the altered check is borne by the bank.	true	false	4.______
5. A bank is liable to the drawer for paying a check on which the payee's indorsement has been forged, but may recover from the holder who presented the check to the bank.	true	false	5.______
6. A bank is in no way liable for any loss that results from its cashing a check that lacks an indorsement.	true	false	6.______
7. Some banks, by express agreement, permit some customers to write checks for more than the amount on deposit.	true	false	7.______
8. A bank can be held liable to a drawer if it pays a postdated check before it is due and such action causes harm to the drawer.	true	false	8.______
9. A bank can be held liable to the payee for wrongfully refusing to pay a check when sufficient funds are on deposit in the bank.	true	false	9.______
10. The drawer of a certified check may issue a stop-payment order on a certified check.	true	false	10.______
11. If, after checking a holder's identification, the bank is suspicious of the holder, it may, without liability to the drawer, refuse to honor the check.	true	false	11.______
12. A drawer who writes a check that a bank dishonors for lack of funds remains liable to a holder.	true	false	12.______
13. A cashier's check is drawn by a bank on its own funds.	true	false	13.______
14. If a bank pays a check that has been materially altered, the bank is not liable to the drawer for the amount of the alteration.	true	false	14.______
15. A bank may pay a check up to 10 days after the death of the drawer.	true	false	15.______

PART 2: For each statement, write the letter of the best answer in the Answers column.

	ANSWERS	*SCORE*
1. A written stop-payment order is effective for (A) fourteen days, (B) seven days, (C) six months, (D) ninety days.	________	1.______
2. A check that a bank draws on its own funds, payable to a certain party, is a (A) cashier's check, (B) certified check, (C) personal check, (D) money order.	________	2.______
3. A personal check that a bank guarantees to pay is a (A) cashier's check, (B) money order, (C) certified check, (D) traveler's check.	________	3.______
4. The relationship between a bank and a depositor who opens a checking account at the bank is one of (A) bailor-bailee, (B) debtor-creditor, (C) bailor-independent contractor, (D) assignor-assignee.	________	4.______
5. If a drawer has a check certified, the drawer (A) remains primarily liable for payment, (B) is relieved of secondary liability, (C) is discharged, (D) remains secondarily liable for payment.	________	5.______

	ANSWERS	SCORE
6. To hold a bank liable for a forged signature, how long does the drawer have after the canceled check has been returned to report the forgery? (A) ninety days, (B) six months, (C) one year, (D) sixty days.	________	6.______
7. If a bank pays a check that has been materially altered, the bank (A) has no liability for the alteration, (B) is liable to the drawer for the amount of the alteration only if the drawer notifies the bank within one year after the altered check is returned to the depositor, (C) is liable only for the original amount of the check, (D) is liable only if notice of the alteration is received by the drawer within one year after the check is returned.	________	7.______
8. The electronic funds transfer system allows depositors (A) to make deposits and withdrawals using a computer terminal, (B) to obtain traveler's checks quickly, (C) to postdate checks, (D) to locate a missing indorsement on a check quickly.	________	8.______
9. A bad check is one written by (A) a maker who has insufficient funds in a savings account, (B) a drawer who has insufficient funds in a checking account, (C) a drawee who has insufficient funds in a checking account, (D) a depositor who has insufficient funds in a savings account.	________	9.______
10. A bank can legally pay or certify checks drawn prior to the drawer's death for how many days after the date of the drawer's death? (A) ninety days, (B) sixty days, (C) five days, (D) ten days.	________	10.______
11. When a depositor tells the bank not to pay a particular check, the procedure is known as (A) dishonoring the check, (B) forging the check, (C) negotiating the check, (D) stopping payment on the check.	________	11.______
12. A postdated check is one that is (A) payable on demand, (B) invalid, (C) payable on its due date, (D) payable 30 days after its due date.	________	12.______
13. A draft issued by a bank, a private company, or the U.S. Postal Service used to transfer funds to a named payee is a (A) money order, (B) certificate of deposit, (C) certified check, (D) stock certificate.	________	13.______
14. When a check is certified, the certifying bank has (A) dishonored the check, (B) drawn on its own funds, (C) guaranteed payment of the check, (D) drawn on the funds in another bank.	________	14.______
15. If the name of a fictitious payee is put on a check and that name is then indorsed, the bank that pays the check (A) is liable for the full amount of the check, (B) is not liable to the drawer, (C) shares liability with the drawer, (D) shares liability with the payee.	________	15.______

PART 3: Answer each of the following questions in the space provided. *SCORE*

1. What responsibilities does a bank have to a depositor for the payment of checks written by the depositor?

____

____ 1.______

2. What liability does a bank have to a depositor for wrongfully refusing to pay a holder the amount of a check written by the depositor?

____

____ 2.______

3. What obligations does a depositor have to the bank in which the depositor maintains a checking account?

____

____ 3.______

NAME ______________________________ DATE ______________

Activity—Writing Checks

Each of the completed checks contains many errors. Study the checks carefully. In the space provided below each check, tell what the errors are. Rewrite each check correctly on the blank forms provided.

Donald E. Swanson
25 Canterbury Lane
Rochester, NY 14643

No. 187

April 31, 19 ― ―   50 – 17 / 223

Pay to the order of ~~Greenwood~~ glenwood Pharmacy $ 8.00

Eighty and 00/100 ~~~~~~~~ Dollars

First Federal Bank of Rochester
Rochester, New York 14643

Dave Swanson

⑆0223⑈0017⑆ 601 428 6⑈

____

____

____

____

____

Donald E. Swanson
25 Canterbury Lane
Rochester, NY 14643

No. 187

__________ 19 ― ―   50 – 17 / 223

Pay to the order of ______________________________ $ ________

______________________________ Dollars

First Federal Bank of Rochester
Rochester, New York 14643

____

⑆0223⑈0017⑆ 601 428 6⑈

Paula Marini
134 North Avenue
Rochester, NY 14643

No. 567

May 15 19 — —

50 – 17
223

Pay to the order of ______________________ $ 40 86/100

Fourty dollars and eighty-six cents ______ Dollars

First Federal Bank of Rochester
Rochester, New York 14643

P. Marini

⑆0223⑈0017⑆ 601 428 6⑈

Paula Marini
134 North Avenue
Rochester, NY 14643

No. 567

______ 19 — —

50 – 17
223

Pay to the order of ______________________ $ ______

______________________________________ Dollars

First Federal Bank of Rochester
Rochester, New York 14643

____

⑆0223⑈0017⑆ 601 428 6⑈

UNIT 7 COMMERCIAL PAPER

Review

NAME________________________ DATE__________

SCORE__________

Review

PART 1: For each statement, write the letter of the best answer in the Answers column.

	ANSWERS	*SCORE*
1. If only the signature of the indorser, ''Mark Hatfield,'' is written on the back of a check, it is known as a(n) (A) bearer indorsement, (B) blank indorsement, (C) order indorsement, (D) special indorsement.	______	1.______
2. To be a holder in due course, a person must take an instrument (A) before its due date, (B) the day after its due date, (C) 30 days after its due date, (D) 10 days after its due date.	______	2.______
3. The party to a draft who is ordered to make payment to the payee is known as the (A) drawer, (B) maker, (C) payer, (D) drawee.	______	3.______
4. The defense that a person was a minor when he or she signed a note is (A) a real defense, (B) an invalid defense, (C) a bearer defense, (D) a personal defense.	______	4.______
5. Defenses that are not good against a holder in due course are known as (A) holder defenses, (B) real defenses, (C) instrument defenses, (D) personal defenses.	______	5.______
6. An indorsement that limits the indorser's liability is called (A) limited, (B) restrictive, (C) qualified, (D) special.	______	6.______
7. To be negotiable, an instrument must be payable in (A) services or money, (B) money only, (C) money or goods, (D) U.S. currency only.	______	7.______
8. The maker of a draft is known as the (A) drawee, (B) payor, (C) drawer, (D) payee.	______	8.______
9. A check that a bank draws on its own funds, payable to a certain party, is called a (A) money order, (B) draft, (C) letter of credit, (D) cashier's check.	______	9.______
10. A check written by a depositor, with the bank's permission, for more than the amount on deposit is called (A) an allonge, (B) an overdraft, (C) a postdated check, (D) a promissory note.	______	10.______
11. When the maker's name on a promissory note has been forged, the maker has a defense that is good against (A) all holders, (B) only ordinary holders, (C) only holders in due course, (D) none of these answers.	______	11.______
12. If there is a discrepancy between the amount written in words and the amount indicated in figures on a check, the amount payable is (A) the amount indicated in figures, (B) the difference between the two amounts, (C) the amount written in words, (D) none of these answers.	______	12.______
13. A promissory note payable in merchandise is (A) negotiable, (B) nonnegotiable, (C) illegal, (D) payable in the dollar equivalent of the merchandise.	______	13.______
14. The maker of a promissory note is an example of a (A) primary party, (B) secondary party, (C) payee, (D) drawee.	______	14.______
15. If a primary party dishonors an instrument, notice of dishonor must be given to the secondary party (A) within 90 days, (B) within 60 days, (C) within a reasonable time, (D) within three business days.	______	15.______
16. A check that is more than six months old is called (A) an overdraft, (B) a stale check, (C) a bad check, (D) a postdated check.	______	16.______

PART 2: Indicate whether each statement below is true or false by circling either "true" or "false" in the Answers column.

	ANSWERS		SCORE
1. A promissory note must contain the letters IOU.	true	false	1.______
2. A negotiable instrument can be readily transferred from one person to another.	true	false	2.______
3. "Payable on demand" means payable when the payee presents it to the person obligated to pay it.	true	false	3.______
4. A bearer instrument may be negotiated by voluntary delivery alone.	true	false	4.______
5. An alteration of commercial paper discharges the obligation of any party whose liability is changed by the alteration.	true	false	5.______
6. Delivery of a note back to the maker cancels the note.	true	false	6.______
7. The liability of secondary parties is unconditional.	true	false	7.______
8. Personal defenses are not good against holders in due course.	true	false	8.______
9. Real defenses make an instrument void from the time of its creation.	true	false	9.______
10. A bank must, without exception, honor all checks written by the depositor.	true	false	10.______
11. A bank may be held liable if it pays a postdated check before its due date.	true	false	11.______
12. A cashier's check is a personal check that a bank guarantees to pay.	true	false	12.______
13. A bank may pay checks for up to 10 days after the drawer's death.	true	false	13.______
14. Presentment is a demand for payment made by or on behalf of a holder.	true	false	14.______
15. A note or check payable in merchandise is a negotiable instrument.	true	false	15.______

PART 3: In the Answers column at the right, write the letter of the word or words in Column 1 that best match each statement in Column 2.

COLUMN 1	*COLUMN 2*	*ANSWERS*	*SCORE*
(A) draft	1. A written promise by one party to pay a certain amount of money to another party.	______	1.______
(B) promissory note	2. Defenses such as fraud or lack of consideration that are not good against holders in due course.	______	2.______
(C) accommodation indorsement	3. An indorsement by a person who helps another by adding her or his signature to guarantee payment.	______	3.______
(D) primary parties	4. A holder who has special rights that can be enforced against a party who is obligated to pay.	______	4.______
(E) dishonor	5. Defenses that exist upon creation of the instrument and are good against all holders.	______	5.______
(F) commercial paper	6. Those persons who are first obligated to make payment on an instrument.	______	6.______
(G) restrictive indorsement	7. An indorsement that limits what a person to whom an instrument is transferred may do with it.	______	7.______
(H) real defenses	8. The different types of written instruments that can be used as a substitute for money.	______	8.______
(I) holder in due course	9. The refusal of the primary party to pay or accept an instrument when it is presented for payment.	______	9.______
(J) personal defenses	10. An order by one party to a second party to pay a certain amount of money to a third party.	______	10.______

PART 4: Answer the following question in the space provided. *SCORE*

What are the advantages of paying for goods and services by check rather than with cash?

____

____

____ ______

UNIT 8 INSURANCE

Chapter 32 Property and Casualty Insurance

NAME________________________ DATE__________

SCORE__________

Study Guide and Review

PART 1: For each statement, write the letter of the best answer in the Answers column. *ANSWERS* *SCORE*

1. A risk or peril specifically not covered by an insurance policy is called an (A) excision, (B) extrusion, (C) exclusion, (D) extension. ________ 1.______
2. The standard fire insurance policy has been adopted in (A) all states west of the Mississippi, (B) all states east of the Mississippi, (C) Alaska and Hawaii only, (D) all states. ________ 2.______
3. Coverage against loss or damage from a windstorm is known as (A) special coverage, (B) extended coverage, (C) windstorm coverage, (D) catastrophe coverage. ________ 3.______
4. To insure property against loss or damage from any cause, you should buy (A) an all-risk policy, (B) a multi-peril policy, (C) a marine policy, (D) a liability policy. ________ 4.______
5. To collect under an insurance policy for damage to property, the insured must have an insurable interest (A) at the time the policy is purchased, (B) at the time the loss occurs, (C) both at the time of purchase and the time of loss, (D) at the time proceeds are paid. ________ 5.______
6. To protect yourself against claims that others might make against you for injuries caused by your negligence and on your property, you need (A) public liability insurance, (B) inland marine insurance, (C) risk insurance, (D) negligence insurance. ________ 6.______
7. An addition to an insurance policy is called (A) a filler, (B) an amendment, (C) a memorandum, (D) a rider. ________ 7.______
8. Most policies protecting residences provide that coverage stops if the residence is vacant for more than (A) 60 days, (B) 30 days, (C) 3 months, (D) 1 year. ________ 8.______
9. The obligation to carry a minimum amount of insurance is called (A) risk sharing, (B) coinsurance, (C) multiple coverage, (D) co-obligation. ________ 9.______
10. An insurance that protects against loss from claims made by persons injured as a result of the insured's actions is (A) fire insurance, (B) public liability insurance, (C) personal liability insurance, (D) standard insurance. ________ 10.______

PART 2: Place a check mark in the Answers column at the right of each statement to indicate whether the risk is covered by a standard fire policy with extended coverage.

	COVERED	*NOT COVERED*	*SCORE*
1. Damage to a roof caused by lightning.	________	________	1.______
2. Breakage of windows as a result of vandalism.	________	________	2.______
3. Damage to a rug due to bursting of a hot water heater.	________	________	3.______
4. Loss of a tree during a windstorm.	________	________	4.______
5. Unexplained disappearance of a camera.	________	________	5.______
6. Smoke damage caused by a kitchen accident.	________	________	6.______
7. Collapse of a roof due to the weight of ice and snow.	________	________	7.______
8. Destruction of your furniture due to a flood.	________	________	8.______
9. A broken window caused by a falling tree branch.	________	________	9.______
10. Damage to your front door during a riot.	________	________	10.______

PART 3: For each of the following case problems, give a decision by writing "yes" or "no" in the space provided. Then, in sentence form, give a reason for your decision.

SCORE

1. Gilbey was burning some leaves in his back yard one afternoon. When he got too close to the flames, his coat caught fire and was ruined. Can he collect from his insurance company under his fire insurance policy for the damage to the coat?

Decision: ______________________________

Reason: ______________________________

______________________________ 1. ______

2. Hanley went to a baseball game and took along a valuable camera. The camera was insured under an all-risk policy. Hanley, through negligence, left the camera in the aisle, where it was stepped on and destroyed. Can Hanley collect from the insurance company for the value of the camera?

Decision: ______________________________

Reason: ______________________________

______________________________ 2. ______

3. Jaffey bought a painting for $2,000 and insured it for that amount. Ten years later, she discovered that the painting was actually a Rembrandt worth two million dollars. If the painting is stolen, can Jaffey collect the full appraised value?

Decision: ______________________________

Reason: ______________________________

______________________________ 3. ______

4. Gregg applied for an insurance policy covering loss of or damage to his motorcycle. In the application, he incorrectly stated the color of his eyes. If the motorcycle is damaged in an accident, can the insurance company refuse to pay for the damage because of the misstatement in the application?

Decision: ______________________________

Reason: ______________________________

____

______________________________ 4. ______

5. Cohen lent Bridges a valuable set of china dishes for use during a party that Bridges was giving at her home. Bridges took out an insurance policy insuring the value of the china. When the china was damaged during the party, Bridges insisted that the insurance company compensate her for the loss. Is she entitled to collect?

Decision: ______________________________

Reason: ______________________________

______________________________ 5. ______

NAME____ DATE______________

6. Davidson insured her jewelry with two insurance agencies. If the jewelry is stolen, can she collect the full policy amount from both agencies?

SCORE

Decision: ____

Reason: ____

____

____

____ 6.______

7. Hughes canceled his car insurance policy before the end of the term. Will Hughes receive a refund for the full amount of the unused premium?

Decision: ____

Reason: ____

____

____

____ 7.______

PART 4: In the Answers column at the right, write the word or words that make each statement correct.

	ANSWERS	*SCORE*
1. A means of sharing risks of loss with others is known as ______.	______	1.______
2. A written insurance contract is called a ______.	______	2.______
3. The greater the risk, the higher will be the ______.	______	3.______
4. An insurance company employee who sells insurance policies only for that company is called an insurance ______.	______	4.______
5. A risk specifically not covered under an insurance policy is called an ______.	______	5.______
6. A policy that states a specific amount to be paid when a loss occurs is said to have ______ coverage.	______	6.______
7. To reduce premiums, insurance companies offer policies containing a ______ clause.	______	7.______
8. A material ______ on an application for an insurance policy may void the policy.	______	8.______
9. In the event of a loss, the first step in presenting the claim is to notify the ______.	______	9.______
10. After a claim is settled, the insured is asked to sign a document called a ______ before payment will be made.	______	10.______

Activity 1—Writing with a Purpose

In the space following the statement below, write a short paragraph in which you agree or disagree with the statement. Give specific reasons for your decision. Be sure to use complete sentences.

SCORE

"All persons should be required by law to carry automobile, health, and life insurance."

____

____

____

____

____

____

____

____

____

____ ______

Activity 2—Word Search

The words listed below describe important terms relating to property and casualty insurance. The words read forward, backward, up, down, and diagonally, but always in a straight line. Circle each word you find.

SCORE

L	R	K	S	I	R	L	L	A	H
R	I	D	E	R	Z	R	B	O	H
V	N	A	P	W	O	E	M	H	P
B	S	W	B	N	L	E	F	O	R
L	U	R	Z	I	O	S	L	M	E
B	R	S	T	W	L	I	O	D	M
C	E	S	N	S	C	I	A	C	I
R	O	E	H	Y	R	H	T	M	U
H	R	T	F	E	H	T	E	Y	M
S	O	C	E	P	O	M	R	G	B

all-risk
floater
homeowners
hostile
insure
liability
policy
premium
rider
theft

______

UNIT 8 INSURANCE

Chapter 33 Automobile Insurance

NAME____________________________________ DATE__________

SCORE__________

Study Guide and Review

PART 1: Indicate whether each statement below is true or false by circling either "true" or "false" in the Answers column.

	ANSWERS		*SCORE*
1. Automobile insurance is compulsory in every state.	true	false	1.______
2. The amount of insurance required varies from state to state.	true	false	2.______
3. Collision insurance pays for damage to a vehicle regardless of who was at fault.	true	false	3.______
4. A deductible feature in an insurance policy usually reduces the amount of the premium.	true	false	4.______
5. Automobile insurance protects the owner only.	true	false	5.______
6. A person's liability for injury to another person is limited to the amount of insurance coverage.	true	false	6.______
7. With no-fault coverage, an injured person may recover from her or his own insurance company regardless of who was at fault.	true	false	7.______
8. All states in the United States have no-fault laws.	true	false	8.______
9. Not all automobile accidents have to be reported to the police.	true	false	9.______
10. An insured may cancel an automobile insurance policy at any time.	true	false	10.______

PART 2: For each statement, write the letter of the best answer in the Answers column.

	ANSWERS	*SCORE*
1. Laws that make sure that owners or drivers are able to pay for damages or injuries caused to others are called (A) coinsurance laws, (B) auto liability laws, (C) financial responsibility laws, (D) no-fault laws.	________	1.______
2. Coverage for injuries caused by a hit-and-run driver is provided by (A) comprehensive insurance, (B) property damage liability insurance, (C) collision insurance, (D) uninsured motorist insurance.	________	2.______
3. The premium for collision insurance can be reduced through (A) coinsurance, (B) a deductible clause, (C) assigned risk, (D) an omnibus clause.	________	3.______
4. In some states, a vehicle owner must provide proof of financial responsibility before the vehicle can be (A) registered, (B) bought, (C) sold, (D) repaired.	________	4.______
5. A person who operates a vehicle with the owner's consent is protected by a clause in an auto insurance policy known as (A) guest, (B) autobus, (C) deductible, (D) omnibus.	________	5.______
6. Cook carries comprehensive insurance on his car. The type of loss or damage to Cook's car that is *not* covered by this insurance is (A) theft, (B) glass breakage, (C) collision, (D) tornado damage.	________	6.______
7. Filing an accident report when there is death or injury is mandatory in (A) all states, (B) those states that have no-fault laws, (C) those states that do not have no-fault laws, (D) none of these answers.	________	7.______
8. If you injure another person in an auto accident and you carry $50,000 of liability insurance, your insurance company is responsible to the extent of (A) $100,000, (B) $50,000, (C) the no-fault threshold figure, (D) whatever the court awards.	________	8.______
9. Guest laws relieve drivers of liability for injuries to guests unless the driver's negligence is (A) average, (B) minimal, (C) gross, (D) zero.	________	9.______

	ANSWERS	SCORE
10. The type of automobile insurance that permits an insured to collect medical expenses resulting from an accident, regardless of fault, is (A) liability, (B) no-fault, (C) comprehensive, (D) collision.	________	10. ______

PART 3: Indicate whether the coverages listed below protect against the risks described in the left column by placing a check mark in the proper column.

	Bodily Injury	Property Damage	Medical Payments	Uninsured Motorist	Collision Coverage	Comprehensive Insurance	SCORE
1. Your car radio is stolen.							1. ______
2. A vandal ruins the finish on your car.							2. ______
3. A falling branch smashes your windshield.							3. ______
4. You back your car into a fire hydrant.							4. ______
5. Your car explodes due to a leak in the gas tank.							5. ______
6. You have to rent a car when yours is stolen.							6. ______
7. A hit-and-run driver hits your car, causing damage.							7. ______
8. You are hospitalized after being in an auto accident.							8. ______
9. Your neighbor sues you after you back into her car.							9. ______
10. You are injured when an unknown driver hits you while you change a tire.							10. ______

PART 4: For each of the following case problems, give a decision by writing "yes" or "no" in the space provided. Then, in sentence form, give a reason for your decision.

SCORE

1. Beatty had collision coverage on her car. While driving to school one day, she made a wrong turn on a one-way street and collided with another car, damaging her own car extensively. Does Beatty have a good claim for this damage?

Decision: ____________________

Reason: ____________________

____________________ 1. ______

2. Cramer bought a new car for $8,000. Two years later, when the car was worth $6,000 and a new one similar to it cost $9,000, it was completely demolished when Cramer drove it into a tree. If Cramer had $250 deductible collision coverage on his car, is the maximum he can collect $5,750?

Decision: ____________________

Reason: ____________________

____________________ 2. ______

UNIT 8 INSURANCE

Chapter 34 Personal Insurance

NAME________________________________ DATE____________

SCORE____________

Study Guide and Review

PART 1: Indicate whether each statement below is true or false by circling either "true" or "false" in the Answers column.

	ANSWERS		*SCORE*
1. An insurance company may require a medical examination before issuing an individual life insurance policy.	true	false	1.______
2. A person owning term insurance cannot borrow the value of the policy.	true	false	2.______
3. An insured person may change the beneficiary of the policy at any time.	true	false	3.______
4. An insurance company can always contest the validity of a policy because of fraud in the application.	true	false	4.______
5. Failure to pay a premium on time always results in cancellation of the policy.	true	false	5.______
6. Group insurance policies are usually less expensive than individual policies.	true	false	6.______
7. Both whole life and term insurance build cash value.	true	false	7.______
8. An insurance company can refuse to pay the policy proceeds if the insured commits suicide at any time during the policy.	true	false	8.______
9. An insured person has the right to assign her or his rights in the life insurance policy.	true	false	9.______
10. A misstatement about age voids an insurance policy.	true	false	10.______
11. Term insurance is more expensive than whole life insurance.	true	false	11.______
12. Term insurance policy premiums usually increase as the insured gets older.	true	false	12.______
13. Life insurance proceeds are always paid in a lump sum.	true	false	13.______
14. An annuity provides insurance protection.	true	false	14.______
15. All insurance policies have premiums that remain the same throughout the term of the policy.	true	false	15.______

PART 2: For each of the following case problems, give a decision by writing "yes" or "no" in the space provided. Then, in sentence form, give a reason for your decision.

SCORE

1. The premium on Benson's life insurance policy was due on December 1. Benson mailed the premium on December 10, but the insurance company refused to accept it, claiming the policy had lapsed. Was the insurance company correct?

Decision: ____

Reason: ____

____ 1.______

2. Harden purchased a life insurance policy. Five years later, he committed suicide. Must the insurance company pay the proceeds of the policy to Harden's beneficiary?

Decision: ____

Reason: ____ 2.______

SCORE

3. On August 1, 1986, Williams submitted a life insurance application to the Premier Life Insurance Co., Inc. Although he was born in 1950, he mistakenly wrote 1960 as his year of birth on the application. If the insurance company discovers the error in Williams's date of birth, can the policy be declared void?

Decision: ______________________________

Reason: ______________________________

______________________________ 3. ______

4. Rustin purchased a 5-year term insurance policy. After 5 years, can Rustin collect the cash value of the policy from the insurance company?

Decision: ______________________________

Reason: ______________________________

______________________________ 4. ______

5. Milton purchased a whole life insurance policy. Several years later, she found she could no longer pay the premiums. Can the insurance company cancel the policy without any further benefit to Milton?

Decision: ______________________________

Reason: ______________________________

____

______________________________ 5. ______

PART 3: In the Answers column at the right, write the letter of the word or words in Column 1 that best match each statement in Column 2.

COLUMN 1	COLUMN 2	ANSWERS	SCORE
(A) group	1. A contract that provides income during the owner's lifetime.	______	1. ______
(B) key-man	2. An insurance policy with a payment schedule having premiums that start out low and increase.	______	2. ______
(C) limited payment	3. A policy insuring all members of a specific group.	______	3. ______
(D) term	4. Insurance purchased by business partners to insure the lives of other partners or stockholders.	______	4. ______
(E) endowment	5. A policy that combines term and permanent insurance to protect the family.	______	5. ______
(F) modified premium	6. Insurance that protects for a limited time.	______	6. ______
(G) annuity	7. Insurance in which premiums are paid for a limited period of time.	______	7. ______
(H) family income	8. Insurance that provides protection until the insured reaches a certain age.	______	8. ______
(I) disability	9. A policy that provides income to an insured person who cannot work because of illness or injury that was caused in an accident.	______	9. ______
(J) whole life	10. A policy offering lifetime protection and premiums that remain the same.	______	10. ______

UNIT 8 INSURANCE

Review

NAME________________________________

DATE____________

SCORE____________

Review

PART 1: Indicate whether each statement below is true or false by writing "true" or "false" in the Answers column.

	ANSWERS		SCORE
1. An insurance broker is employed by an insurance company to sell insurance.	true	false	1.______
2. An insurance company will not issue a policy without an application.	true	false	2.______
3. Once an insured makes the first premium payment, the insurance company is obligated on the policy regardless of the presence of an insurable interest.	true	false	3.______
4. If an insured person suffers a loss that equals the deductible amount, the insured will not recover anything from the insurance company.	true	false	4.______
5. An insurance company may cancel a policy because of false information in the application even if it didn't rely on the information in issuing the policy.	true	false	5.______
6. Fire insurance does not cover smoke damage caused by a fire.	true	false	6.______
7. A homeowners policy covers damage to personal property of guests while they are on the insured's property.	true	false	7.______
8. Specific coverage in a property insurance policy becomes a problem if costs rise because of inflation.	true	false	8.______
9. An insurance company may cancel an insurance policy if the insured increases the risk of loss or damage.	true	false	9.______
10. A passenger in a car who shares the expenses of a trip is not protected by an automobile guest law.	true	falsc	10.______

PART 2: In the Answers column at the right, write the letter of the word or words in Column 1 that best match each statement in Column 2.

COLUMN 1	*COLUMN 2*	*ANSWERS*	*SCORE*
(A) coinsurance	1. That part of a loss paid for by the insured.	________	1.______
(B) short rate	2. A legal form signed when a claim is settled.	________	2.______
(C) subrogation	3. Laws that define responsibility toward passengers in the insured's car.	________	3.______
(D) binder	4. An insurance policy clause requiring an insured to maintain a certain amount of insurance.	________	4.______
(E) indemnification	5. An insurance company's right to recover from the person responsible for the loss.	________	5.______
(F) proximate cause	6. A temporary policy issued before a permanent policy is issued.	________	6.______
(G) release	7. Compensation to an insured for loss of or damage to insured property.	________	7.______
(H) guest laws	8. The premium amount refunded to the insured when a policy is canceled by the insurer.	________	8.______
(I) floater	9. An all-risk policy that covers loss or damage to personal property from any cause.	________	9.______
(J) deductible	10. The direct or natural cause of loss or damage.	________	10.______

PART 3: For each statement, write the letter of the best answer in the Answers column.

	ANSWERS	SCORE
1. Insurance may be issued by (A) department stores, (B) savings banks, (C) churches and synagogues, (D) city governments.	______	1. ______
2. An insurance salesperson who sells insurance issued by several companies is an (A) insurance agent, (B) issuer, (C) actuary, (D) insurance broker.	______	2. ______
3. When an insurance company does not give a binder, a policy becomes effective when (A) the application is received, (B) the application is accepted, (C) 30 days have gone by, (D) the policy is delivered to the insured.	______	3. ______
4. If an insured does not have an insurable interest in the life or the property insured, (A) the policy is void, (B) the policy is voidable at the insured's option, (C) the insured may collect only half the face value, (D) the insured cannot recover any premiums paid.	______	4. ______
5. If you own a painting valued at $5,000 and want to guarantee payment of that amount in the event of theft, regardless of the actual value at the time of the loss, you should select insurance with (A) inflation coverage, (B) open coverage, (C) valued coverage, (D) closed coverage.	______	5. ______
6. To be fully protected from loss of or damage to personal property from any reason, you would select (A) an all-risk policy, (B) a homeowners policy, (C) a multi-peril policy, (D) a standard policy.	______	6. ______
7. If a person insures property with more than one company and a loss occurs, (A) the company that issued the first policy is liable for the loss, (B) neither company is liable, (C) each company will pay its pro-rata share of the loss, (D) each company must pay the full amount of the loss.	______	7. ______
8. Property and casualty policies may be canceled (A) when a loss occurs, (B) at any time by the insured or the insurer, (C) by the insured only, (D) by the insurer only.	______	8. ______
9. An insured who has property and casualty insurance (A) may assign the policy at any time, (B) is prohibited from assigning the policy, (C) may assign the policy with the consent of the insurance company, (D) can only assign the policy before a loss occurs.	______	9. ______
10. Collision insurance insures against (A) injury to the insured, (B) damage to another's car, (C) injury to another person, (D) damage to the insured's car.	______	10. ______
11. The coverage under a policy in which a specific amount is payable is called (A) closed, (B) specific, (C) open, (D) valued.	______	11. ______
12. Concealing material information on an insurance application (A) voids the policy, (B) makes the policy voidable at the insurance company's option, (C) has no effect on the policy, (D) has no effect if the initial premium has been paid.	______	12. ______
13. To insure a 35 mm camera against any type of loss, you would purchase a (A) theft policy, (B) homeowners policy, (C) comprehensive policy, (D) floater policy.	______	13. ______
14. Insurance coverage that pays for damage if a driver loses control of her or his car and crashes into a store window is (A) comprehensive, (B) property damage, (C) collision, (D) public liability.	______	14. ______
15. Ward, age 40, wants to insure his life. To receive the face value of the policy when he reaches age 60, he should buy (A) a term policy, (B) a 20-year endowment policy, (C) a 20-payment life policy, (D) an annuity with payments beginning at age 60.	______	15. ______
16. Upon the insured's death, the life insurance company pays (A) the face value of the policy to the beneficiary, (B) the cash surrender value to the beneficiary, (C) the face value to the insured, (D) the cash surrender value to the insured.	______	16. ______
17. Hubbard planned to fly from Boston to Dallas. She purchased a life insurance policy that covered her solely during the trip. Such a policy is known as (A) a straight life policy, (B) a term policy, (C) an endowment policy, (D) an annuity.	______	17. ______
18. A life insurance company may avoid paying the face amount of the policy if the insured commits suicide (A) before age 18, (B) before age 21, (C) within the first two policy years, (D) within the first three policy years.	______	18. ______

UNIT 9 REAL AND PERSONAL PROPERTY

Chapter 35 Real and Personal Property

NAME________________________________ DATE____________

SCORE____________

Study Guide and Review

PART 1: Indicate whether each statement below is true or false by circling either "true" or "false" in the Answers column.

	ANSWERS		*SCORE*
1. A patent is not considered personal property because it represents only a right to property and not property itself.	true	false	1.______
2. A public utility that wants a permanent right to cross someone's property with a power line will secure an easement for that purpose.	true	false	2.______
3. Both real and personal property may be acquired by inheritance.	true	false	3.______
4. A person who occupies land belonging to another person for a certain period of time may claim title to the land under a right known as prescription.	true	false	4.______
5. Title by adverse possession is obtainable only if the other person's property was occupied through error.	true	false	5.______
6. If two or more persons own property jointly, the property will automatically belong to the survivor(s) upon death of one of the owners.	true	false	6.______
7. The distinguishing feature of a tenancy in common is the right of survivorship.	true	false	7.______
8. Zoning of land for certain uses may only be accomplished with the consent of the owner.	true	false	8.______
9. Title to public property may not be acquired through adverse possession.	true	false	9.______
10. A restrictive covenant ends when the property is sold to a new owner.	true	false	10.______

PART 2: For each statement, write the letter of the best answer in the Answers column.

	ANSWERS	*SCORE*
1. Patent and copyright protection is granted by (A) state governments, (B) a warranty, (C) the Chamber of Commerce, (D) the federal government.	________	1.______
2. A patent protects an inventor for (A) 10 years, (B) 17 years, (C) 35 years, (D) 37 years.	________	2.______
3. Ownership of property by one person is known as (A) tenancy in common, (B) tenancy by the entirety, (C) a cooperative, (D) sole tenancy.	________	3.______
4. Upon the death of a joint tenant, the property automatically belongs to the (A) surviving joint tenants, (B) state, (C) spouse, (D) heirs.	________	4.______
5. The use of land may be restricted by (A) the state government, (B) the federal government, (C) the city government, (D) all of these answers.	________	5.______
6. The process by which the state may obtain title to abandoned or unclaimed property is called (A) presumption, (B) adverse possession, (C) condemnation, (D) escheat.	________	6.______
7. An example of a "fixture" is (A) a refrigerator, (B) an elevator, (C) a typewriter, (D) a couch.	________	7.______
8. The temporary right to use a portion of another person's land is known as (A) a profit, (B) an easement, (C) a permit, (D) a license.	________	8.______
9. Ownership of a condominium unit is shown by a (A) stock certificate, (B) mortgage, (C) bill of sale, (D) deed.	________	9.______
10. A restrictive covenant is binding on (A) the seller, (B) the original buyer, (C) the neighbors, (D) all subsequent buyers.	________	10.______

PART 3: In the Answers column at the right, write the letter of the word or words in Column 1 that best match each statement in Column 2.

COLUMN 1	COLUMN 2	ANSWERS	SCORE
(A) condominium	1. The right to use someone's property perpetually or for a specific period of time.	______	1. ______
(B) easement	2. The process by which a state government obtains title to private property that is abandoned or unclaimed.	______	2. ______
(C) escheat	3. A word or symbol used to identify a product or a business.	______	3. ______
(D) adverse possession	4. A temporary right to use someone's property, cancelable at any time.	______	4. ______
(E) license	5. Ownership of a specific unit in an apartment project.	______	5. ______
(F) restrictive covenant	6. A clause in a deed restricting the use of property.	______	6. ______
(G) trademark	7. Occupying another person's land without that person's permission.	______	7. ______
(H) fixture	8. A grant to a person of an exclusive right to manufacture and sell, or license others to make and sell, an invention.	______	8. ______
(I) deed	9. An item of personal property attached to and treated as real property.	______	9. ______
(J) patent	10. A formal document transferring title to real property.	______	10. ______

PART 4: Answer each of the following questions in the space provided. *SCORE*

1. Explain the difference between a joint tenancy and a tenancy in common.

____

____

____

____

____ 1. ______

2. Explain the nature of patents, copyrights, and trademarks and the type of protection afforded by each.

____

____

____

____

____ 2. ______

3. List the different ways in which real property may be acquired.

____

____

____ 3. ______

UNIT 9 REAL AND PERSONAL PROPERTY

Chapter 36 Landlord and Tenant

NAME_______________________________ DATE__________

SCORE__________

Study Guide and Review

PART 1: For each statement, write the letter of the best answer in the Answers column. *ANSWERS* *SCORE*

1. Under the statute of frauds, a lease of real property must be in writing if it is for (A) residential property, (B) commercial property, (C) more than one year, (D) less than one year. ________ 1.______
2. The major difference among the various types of tenancies is (A) the relationship between the parties, (B) the length of the lease term, (C) the type of property being leased, (D) the rent to be paid under the lease. ________ 2.______
3. To rent property for an indefinite time so that you can cancel the lease at any time, you should get a (A) tenancy at will, (B) hold-over tenancy, (C) tenancy at sufferance, (D) periodic tenancy. ________ 3.______
4. When a lease is assigned by a tenant, (A) the original tenant has no further obligations, (B) the landlord assumes all responsibility, (C) the new tenant assumes all responsibility, (D) the original tenant is still liable. ________ 4.______
5. Most leases provide that if the leased property is totally destroyed by fire or other casualty, (A) rent continues, (B) the tenant pays half the original rent, (C) the lease terminates, (D) the tenant pays the cost of repairs. ________ 5.______
6. Graber is renting an apartment to Brill. Graber can require Brill to pay a security deposit to be used to (A) pay the first month's rent, (B) pay for damage caused during Brill's lease term, (C) pay the last month's rent, (D) pay property taxes. ________ 6.______
7. Under most leases, permanent fixtures installed by the tenant (A) may be removed by the tenant when the lease ends, (B) become the property of the landlord and may not be removed, (C) must be purchased by the landlord when the lease ends, (D) belong to the next tenant. ________ 7.______
8. If a tenant fails to pay the rent when it becomes due, the landlord may (A) sue to evict the tenant, (B) sue the tenant for the balance of the rent, (C) have the tenant arrested, (D) evict and/or sue the tenant. ________ 8.______
9. A constructive eviction occurs when (A) the landlord wants to repair the property, (B) the tenant redecorates the property without the landlord's permission, (C) the landlord makes the property uninhabitable, (D) the tenant intentionally damages or destroys the property. ________ 9.______
10. A person who leases residential property (A) may be restricted in the type of furniture placed on the property, (B) may be restricted from having visitors, (C) may use the property only for the purpose described in the lease, (D) may use the property for any purpose. ________ 10.______
11. A landlord's promise in a lease that the tenant will have undisturbed possession of the property is known as a (A) covenant of quiet enjoyment, (B) tenancy at sufferance, (C) constructive eviction, (D) warranty of habitability. ________ 11.______
12. A lease that omits the names of the landlord or tenant is (A) enforceable, (B) a sublease, (C) unenforceable, (D) a covenant. ________ 12.______

PART 2: Answer the following questions in the space provided. SCORE

1. Explain the difference between a lease and a sublease.

____

____

____

____ 1.______

2. List seven important terms that every lease should contain.

 1. ____
 2. ____
 3. ____
 4. ____
 5. ____
 6. ____
 7. ____ 2.______

3. Describe four ways in which a lease may be terminated.

____

____

____

____ 3.______

Activity 1—Word Search

The 10 words listed below describe important terms relating to landlord-tenant relationships. The words read forward, backward, up, down, and diagonally, but always in a straight line and never skipping a letter. Circle each word you find. SCORE

T	E	N	A	N	C	Y	X	C	S
E	S	A	E	L	O	E	F	T	U
R	E	R	K	T	V	T	E	U	B
Z	C	A	N	H	E	N	V	H	L
Y	U	E	E	N	N	C	I	R	E
F	R	B	A	E	A	B	C	G	A
G	I	N	F	T	N	J	T	Y	S
H	T	E	R	U	T	X	I	F	E
A	Y	C	L	I	S	A	O	M	S
B	S	D	R	O	L	D	N	A	L

covenants
eviction
fixture
landlord
lease
rent
security
sublease
tenancy
tenant

______

NAME ______________________ DATE ____________

Activity 2—Analyzing a Lease

Read the following lease and then answer the questions on the next page.

LEASE

THIS INDENTURE WITNESSETH, That Mark and Anna Essex of the County of Marion in the State of Indiana has this day leased to Brent J. and LeeAnn McDowell, of said County and State, and to their executor/executrix, administrator/administratrix, and assigns the following premises in said County and State, to-wit:

Condominium #15A located in Valley Vista Estates, 2062 West Park Drive, Southport, Indiana, consisting of five (5) rooms plus bath, garage, and patio,

together with the right, privileges, and appurtenances to the same belonging, to have and to hold the same for and during the term of one (1) year from the 1st day of April, 19--. And the said Brent J. and LeeAnn McDowell hereby agree___ to pay as rent for said premises, the sum of Two Hundred Fifty Dollars ($250.00) per month, the said rent to be paid on the 2nd day of each month in advance without relief from valuation or appraisement laws. THE CONDITIONS of this lease are: That the premises are to be used and occupied by Brent J. and LeeAnn McDowell for a residence and for no other purpose. That no waste be allowed to accumulate on the premises. That the premises are not to be sub-leased by said Brent J. and LeeAnn McDowell or occupied by other persons or for other purposes than herein expressed, or this lease assigned by the said Brent J. and LeeAnn McDowell without the written consent of the said Mark and Anna Essex

And the said lessee hereby further agree______, at the expiration of this lease to deliver up the possession of said premises, peaceable and in as good condition and repair as the same is now in, or in as good condition and repair as the said lessor may at any time during this lease put the same in. The natural wear, accidents, fire, and other acts of God excepted.

At the expiration of this lease, or on the failure to pay the rent when the same is due, or on a failure to comply with any of the conditions of this lease, the same shall terminate at once without notice, and the said Mark and Anna Essex representatives and assigns may enter upon and take possession of said premises and expel the occupants thereof, without in anywise being a trespasser; and the failure of the said Mark and Anna Essex to take possession of said premises at the times aforesaid, shall not estop them from afterwards asserting said rights, and the occupation of said premises by the said tenant, after the expiration of said lease, or the forteiture thereof, shall give them no rights as a tenant but they may be expelled at any time without notice. On failure to pay rent at maturity, or to give possession at the expiration of this lease and as liquidated damages for failure, it is agreed that double the rent above specified shall be paid for the time the rent remains due or unpaid or said tenant holds possession without right, and should suit be instituted to collect rent, or obtain possession of the said premises, the said Brent J. and LeeAnn McDowell agrees to pay attorney's fees therefor.

Witness our hands, this 10th day of March, 19--

Mark Essex	*Brent J. McDowell*
Mark Essex	Brent J. McDowell
Anna Essex	*LeeAnn McDowell*
Anna Essex	LeeAnn McDowell

THIS DOCUMENT PREPARED BY Anthony E. Santos, QUIMBY, SANTOS & LOUIS

1. Who is the landlord? ______ SCORE

Who is the tenant? ______ 1. ______

2. What is the term of this lease? ______ 2. ______

3. What type of tenancy is provided for with this lease? ______

______ 3. ______

4. What are the restrictions on the use of this property outlined in the lease?

______

______

______ 4. ______

5. If the tenants fail to pay the rent, what damages are provided for in the lease?

______

______

______ 5. ______

6. Under this lease, who is responsible for paying the real estate taxes? Why?

______

______

______ 6. ______

7. Under the lease, how may the tenants sublease this property? ______

______ 7. ______

8. What are the obligations of the tenants at the end of the term of this lease?

______

______ 8. ______

9. If a fire destroys part of the kitchen during the term of this lease, who is responsible for having the damages repaired? Why?

______

______

______ 9. ______

10. If the tenants are sued for failure to pay the rent or to vacate the property at the end of the term of the lease, who must pay the attorneys' fees?

______ 10. ______

UNIT 9 REAL AND PERSONAL PROPERTY

Chapter 37 Buying a Home

NAME________________________ DATE__________

SCORE__________

Study Guide and Review

PART 1: Indicate whether each statement below is true or false by circling either "true" or "false" in the Answers column.

	ANSWERS		SCORE
1. A contract for the sale and purchase of a home need not be in writing if the purchase price is under $25,000.	true	false	1.______
2. A homeowner and a potential buyer may negotiate directly, without using the services of a real estate broker.	true	false	2.______
3. Once a contract of sale is executed, it is binding on both seller and buyer.	true	false	3.______
4. Contingencies in a contract protect the buyer but not the seller.	true	false	4.______
5. In buying a house with a mortgage already on it, the buyer may always assume the mortgage without the mortgagee's consent.	true	false	5.______
6. The seller may give a mortgage to the buyer in the same way that a lending institution can give a mortgage.	true	false	6.______
7. Every mortgage gives the mortgagor the right to pay the balance due on the mortgage, without penalty, before the end of the mortgage term.	true	false	7.______
8. When a house is sold, the buyer pays the real estate agent's commission.	true	false	8.______
9. Title insurance protects the buyer against any resulting financial loss if the title proves to be defective.	true	false	9.______
10. Title to real estate passes from seller to buyer when the deed is recorded in the appropriate public office.	true	false	10.______

PART 2: In the Answers column at the right, write the letter of the word or words in Column 1 that best match each statement in Column 2.

COLUMN 1	COLUMN 2	ANSWERS	SCORE
(A) abstract of title	1. A mortgage used to finance the purchase of real property.	________	1.______
(B) counteroffer	2. The holding of closing documents and purchase funds until a title search is made.	________	2.______
(C) covenants	3. A summary of transactions concerning the title to real property.	________	3.______
(D) escrow	4. The legal interest an owner has in real property.	________	4.______
(E) grantee	5. A counter-proposal made by a seller to the offer made by a buyer to purchase real property.	________	5.______
(F) mortgage commitment	6. A deed given by the seller to the buyer that guarantees good title.	________	6.______
(G) purchase money mortgage	7. Promises made by a grantor in a warranty deed.	________	7.______
(H) quitclaim deed	8. A deed that gives to the buyer whatever title the seller had.	________	8.______
(I) title	9. An agreement by a lending institution to give a mortgage to the mortgagor.	________	9.______
(J) warranty deed	10. The person to whom title is transferred by the owner of real property.	________	10.______

PART 3: For each statement, write the letter of the best answer in the Answers column. *ANSWERS* *SCORE*

1. A contract entered into between a property owner and a broker for the sale of real property is known as (A) an oral contract, (B) a listing contract, (C) a title contract, (D) a deed contract. ________ 1.______
2. Ownership of real property is transferred by means of (A) a mortgage, (B) title insurance, (C) a deed, (D) a bond. ________ 2.______
3. A provision in a contract of sale that makes the sale subject to obtaining financing is known as (A) a covenant, (B) a restriction, (C) an easement, (D) a contingency. ________ 3.______
4. When a buyer takes over and agrees to pay an existing mortgage, the process is known as (A) a prepayment privilege, (B) escrow, (C) mortgage assumption, (D) a purchase offer. ________ 4.______
5. A survey that shows approximate measurements taken with a measuring tape is called (A) a tape location map, (B) an instrument survey, (C) a plot, (D) a transit. ________ 5.______
6. A person who transfers real estate to another is known as the (A) grantor, (B) mortgagor, (C) mortgagee, (D) grantee. ________ 6.______
7. The most thorough interest in real property is obtained by receiving a (A) mortgage, (B) warranty deed, (C) quitclaim deed, (D) bargain and sale deed. ________ 7.______
8. To ensure that title to real property is good, a buyer may purchase (A) mortgage insurance, (B) homeowners insurance, (C) title insurance, (D) liability insurance. ________ 8.______
9. To determine whether title to property is good, an attorney usually uses (A) a computer, (B) a deed to the property, (C) an abstract of title, (D) a survey. ________ 9.______
10. Claims against property for unpaid taxes, claims of a mortgagee, and so forth are known as (A) covenants, (B) prescriptions, (C) escrows, (D) encumbrances. ________ 10.______
11. Conditions included in a contract of sale that, if not met, may void the agreement are known as (A) contingencies, (B) covenants, (C) encumbrances, (D) escrow. ________ 11.______
12. A lien held by a bank or other lender as security until a loan for the purchase of property is repaid is called (A) a title, (B) a mortgage, (C) escrow, (D) a deed. ________ 12.______
13. A property survey made by a surveyor that shows exact angles and distances is known as (A) a tape location map, (B) the Torrens system, (C) a title search, (D) an instrument survey. ________ 13.______
14. A copy or condensed summary of all transactions relating to a particular piece of property over a period of years is called (A) a deed, (B) an abstract of title, (C) a closing statement, (D) a listing contract. ________ 14.______
15. Promises and guarantees transferred by a warranty deed are called (A) covenants, (B) contingencies, (C) escrow, (D) surveys. ________ 15.______

PART 4: The following statements contain language taken from various deeds. In the space provided, state what type of deed was used. *SCORE*

1. The grantor hereby gives to the grantee whatever title the grantor may have in and to the following property.

   Type of deed: ____ 1.______

2. The grantor hereby gives to the grantee whatever title the grantor may have in and to the following property and covenants that the grantor is in possession of the property and has done nothing to harm or disturb the title to the property.

   Type of deed: ____ 2.______

3. The grantor hereby gives to the grantee all of the rights to the following property and covenants to forever warrant the title to the property.

   Type of deed: ____ 3.______

UNIT 9 REAL AND PERSONAL PROPERTY

Review

NAME____________________ DATE__________

SCORE__________

Review

PART 1: For each statement, write the letter of the best answer in the Answers column. *ANSWERS* *SCORE*

1. A promissory note is an example of (A) real property, (B) intangible personal property, (C) fixed property, (D) tangible personal property. ________ 1.______
2. A trailer is considered (A) personal property, (B) real property, (C) real and personal property, (D) none of these answers. ________ 2.______
3. If you want a permanent right to cross your neighbor's land to have access to a lake, you would try to get (A) a license, (B) a profit, (C) a patent, (D) an easement. ________ 3.______
4. Real property, but not personal property, may be transferred by (A) gift, (B) deed, (C) purchase, (D) inheritance. ________ 4.______
5. A bill of sale would be used to transfer title to (A) a cottage and lakefront lot, (B) a car, (C) a farm, (D) a home. ________ 5.______
6. A covenant restricting the use of land may be imposed by (A) local or state government, (B) the federal government, (C) local, state, or federal government, (D) none of these. ________ 6.______
7. Permitting your neighbor to store her sailboat on your property for a certain period of time is considered (A) a license, (B) an easement, (C) a profit, (D) a tenancy. ________ 7.______
8. The law requiring that a lease of real property for more than one year be in writing is known as the (A) statute of limitations, (B) law of 1879, (C) statute of writings, (D) statute of frauds. ________ 8.______
9. An escalator clause in a lease is designed to protect the (A) tenant, (B) state government, (C) federal government, (D) landlord. ________ 9.______
10. At the end of a lease term, any security deposit is usually given to the (A) tenant, (B) landlord, (C) new tenant, (D) Housing Authority. ________ 10.______
11. To lease property for a specific period of time and have the lease continue automatically unless you or your landlord cancels it, you would get (A) a tenancy at will, (B) a joint tenancy, (C) a periodic tenancy, (D) a tenancy at sufferance. ________ 11.______
12. If government condemns property for public use, it must pay the owner (A) the property's fair value, (B) whatever the owner paid for the property, (C) double the market value, (D) one half the market value. ________ 12.______
13. A lease may be terminated by (A) agreement between parties, (B) the passage of time, (C) destruction of the property, (D) all of these answers. ________ 13.______
14. A landlord may permit a tenant to secure another occupant of the premises leased by means of (A) an eviction, (B) a sublease, (C) a novation, (D) an accord and satisfaction. ________ 14.______
15. Title to real property passes to the buyer (A) when the purchase price is paid, (B) when the deed is recorded, (C) when a deposit is given, (D) when the deed is delivered. ________ 15.______
16. At the closing, the buyer and seller and their attorneys meet for the purpose of (A) surveying the property, (B) considering a purchase offer, (C) transferring title, (D) conducting a title search. ________ 16.______

PART 2: Indicate whether each statement below is true or false by circling either "true" or "false" in the Answers column.

	ANSWERS		SCORE
1. A patent protects an inventor for a lifetime.	true	false	1. ______
2. A copyright protects any form of expression except musical compositions.	true	false	2. ______
3. To transfer real property as a gift, a deed must be signed and delivered.	true	false	3. ______
4. An appliance can usually be removed from a home prior to sale, provided it does not damage the real property.	true	false	4. ______
5. Title to public property may be acquired through adverse possession.	true	false	5. ______
6. A person who owns land may prohibit its future sale to persons of certain nationalities.	true	false	6. ______
7. The purchaser of a cooperative apartment receives a separate deed indicating ownership of the unit.	true	false	7. ______
8. Government may restrict the use of land to aid the public welfare.	true	false	8. ______
9. Under certain circumstances, a state may claim ownership of property if it has been abandoned or unclaimed for a certain period of time.	true	false	9. ______
10. In most states, title to property held in the names of two or more persons is a tenancy by the entirety.	true	false	10. ______
11. The landlord's and tenant's obligations in a lease are known as warranties.	true	false	11. ______
12. If leased premises are partially destroyed by fire and can be repaired, the lease will continue while repairs are made.	true	false	12. ______
13. If the entire leased premises are taken by condemnation, the tenant is entitled to finish out the remainder of the lease.	true	false	13. ______
14. The bargain and sale deed transfers whatever title the seller has in the property but does not guarantee that the seller has done nothing to disturb the title.	true	false	14. ______
15. If a lease is assigned, the assignee becomes a tenant of the assignor.	true	false	15. ______
16. If a guest is injured on leased premises, the landlord and tenant may be held liable for the guest's injuries.	true	false	16. ______
17. If a buyer of a home assumes a mortgage covering the property, the seller is released from liability on the mortgage.	true	false	17. ______
18. A husband and wife who own property as tenants by the entirety cannot sell their individual interests without the consent of the other.	true	false	18. ______
19. A buyer may refuse to complete the purchase of a home if it is discovered that there are flaws in the title.	true	false	19. ______
20. A guarantee of title is one of the covenants in a bargain and sale deed.	true	false	20. ______

PART 3: In the Answers column at the right, write the letter of the word or words in Column 1 that best match each statement in Column 2.

COLUMN 1

(A) purchase money mortgage
(B) sublease
(C) encumbrance
(D) escheat
(E) escrow
(F) tenancy at will
(G) title
(H) constructive eviction
(I) profit
(J) sole tenancy

COLUMN 2	ANSWERS	SCORE
1. A state's obtaining title to abandoned property.	______	1. ______
2. The right to remove water, gas, minerals, and wood from someone else's property.	______	2. ______
3. Ownership by one person.	______	3. ______
4. A lease of real property for an indefinite period.	______	4. ______
5. A transfer by a tenant of a portion of an unexpired lease term.	______	5. ______
6. Conduct by a landlord making the leased premises uninhabitable by the tenant.	______	6. ______
7. A mortgage obtained by a buyer to finance the purchase of real property.	______	7. ______
8. The holding of closing documents and funds in trust until it is determined the title is clear.	______	8. ______
9. The interest a person has in real property.	______	9. ______
10. An interest in real property that conflicts with the owner's title.	______	10. ______

UNIT 10 WILLS AND ESTATE PLANNING

Chapter 38 Wills and Intestacy

NAME______________________ DATE__________

SCORE__________

Study Guide and Review

PART 1: For each statement, write the letter of the best answer in the Answers column. *ANSWERS* *SCORE*

1. The estate of a person who dies without a will is distributed according to (A) federal law, (B) oral instructions given by the person before death, (C) state law, (D) the customs of the area where the person lived. ________ 1.______
2. Property owned by joint tenants with right of survivorship is distributed upon one tenant's death (A) according to that person's will, (B) to the survivor(s), (C) according to state law, (D) to that person's children. ________ 2.______
3. In most states, a valid will may be executed by (A) a person of any age, (B) a person under 16, (C) a person over 25, (D) a person 18 or over. ________ 3.______
4. To be valid, a written will may be (A) typed, (B) handwritten, (C) printed, (D) any of these answers. ________ 4.______
5. A completely handwritten will is called a (A) nuncupative will, (B) holographic will, (C) xerographic will, (D) de minimus will. ________ 5.______
6. In most states a will, to be valid, must be signed by the testator (A) at the beginning of the will, (B) after the witnesses' signatures, (C) on each page, (D) at the end of the will. ________ 6.______
7. Of the following methods, the only one that does not effectively revoke a will is (A) executing a codicil, (B) sending a letter of revocation to one's heirs, (C) writing a new will, (D) destroying the old will. ________ 7.______
8. In most states, the number of witnesses required for a will to be valid is (A) one, (B) four, (C) two or three, (D) five. ________ 8.______
9. Persons named as beneficiaries in a will (A) may witness the will, (B) may not witness the will, (C) should witness the will, (D) may witness the will if they are over 18. ________ 9.______
10. The person named in a will to carry out its terms is the (A) guardian, (B) spouse, (C) administrator, (D) executor. ________ 10.______

PART 2: In the Answers column at the right, write the word or words that make each statement correct. *ANSWERS* *SCORE*

1. A person who makes a will is called a ______. ________________ 1.______
2. A person who dies without a will is said to have died ______. ________________ 2.______
3. Establishing a will's validity is a process called ______. ________________ 3.______
4. The ______ is the person who handles the estate of a person who dies without a will. ________________ 4.______
5. In most states, a person who is entitled to share in the estate of a person who dies intestate is called an ______. ________________ 5.______
6. An oral will made in the presence of witnesses is a ______. ________________ 6.______
7. A ______ is an amendment to a will. ________________ 7.______
8. The first step in making a will is to consult an ______. ________________ 8.______
9. A gift of personal property by will is known as a ______. ________________ 9.______
10. The right of a ______ to receive a certain portion of an estate cannot be defeated by a will's provisions. ________________ 10.______

PART 3: Read the following will and answer the questions that follow.

I, Sam Taylor, declare that this is my will:

1. I give my wife the sum of $10 as she has enough money of her own to provide for her needs.
2. I devise my half of the home I own jointly with my wife to my good friend, Robert Fisk.
3. I bequeath the sum of $100,000 to the American Cancer Society.
4. I leave the balance of my estate, consisting of $400,000 in real estate, to my children, Janet and Mark Taylor.

Sam Taylor
____

The above will was signed by Sam Taylor in our presence and was declared by him to be his last will. He asked us to act as witnesses and we now sign this will as witnesses to it.

Janet Taylor ________ residing at 93 Providence Rd., Reston, Virginia

Mark Taylor ________ residing at 1628 Harrison Street, Akron, Ohio.

	ANSWERS	SCORE
1. Must Sam's wife accept the $10 as the only amount she is entitled to from his estate?	________	1. ____
2. May Robert Fisk acquire good title to the house under Paragraph 2 of the will?	________	2. ____
3. Is the will invalid because Sam typed his name at the end instead of signing it?	________	3. ____
4. Is the provision in Paragraph 3 of the will valid?	________	4. ____
5. If Sam left $100,000 to the U.S. government as a contribution, would such a provision be held valid?	________	5. ____
6. If Sam's wife had died before he did, would Robert Fisk get valid title to Sam's home?	________	6. ____
7. Will the gifts to Sam's children be held valid?	________	7. ____
8. If Sam had left nothing to his children, would that alone have made the will invalid?	________	8. ____
9. Is the will considered valid without a notary's acknowledgment of Sam's signature?	________	9. ____
10. Would this will have been valid if Sam had been 17 years old when he prepared it?	________	10. ____

Activity—Preparing a Will

A blank form of a will is provided on the next page. Using the information you learned in this chapter, make up your own will.

Last Will and Testament

UNIT 10 WILLS AND ESTATE PLANNING

Chapter 39 Estate Planning

NAME________________________ DATE__________

SCORE__________

Study Guide and Review

PART 1: For each statement, write the letter of the best answer in the Answers column.

	ANSWERS	SCORE
1. An estate tax is imposed by (A) all states, (B) the federal government, (C) the banks, (D) each city.	________	1.______
2. The major reason for estate planning is (A) to create an estate, (B) to provide liquidity, (C) to minimize taxes, (D) all of these answers.	________	2.______
3. The federal estate tax is a tax on (A) the gross estate, (B) the marital deduction, (C) the net estate, (D) trusts.	________	3.______
4. A trust set up in one's will is called (A) an inter vivos trust, (B) a living trust, (C) a Clifford trust, (D) a testamentary trust.	________	4.______
5. The marital deduction allows property to pass to a surviving spouse tax-free (A) up to \$100,000, (B) over \$100,000, (C) in an unlimited amount, (D) over \$250,000.	________	5.______
6. Each year, a married couple may jointly give tax-free gifts to individuals in the amount of (A) \$6,000, (B) \$12,000, (C) \$10,000, (D) \$20,000.	________	6.______
7. The person who receives benefits from a trust is known as the (A) settlor, (B) heir, (C) beneficiary, (D) trustor.	________	7.______
8. Information needed for successful estate planning includes (A) social security numbers, (B) family history, (C) insurance policy information, (D) all of these answers.	________	8.______
9. The main advantage of a testamentary trust is (A) reduced income taxes, (B) reduced estate taxes, (C) flexibility, (D) liquidity.	________	9.______
10. Property that qualifies for the marital deduction includes (A) jointly held real estate, (B) insurance proceeds payable to a spouse, (C) jointly owned stocks, (D) all of these.	________	10.______

PART 2: In the Answers column at the right, write the letter of the word or words in Column 1 that best match each statement in Column 2.

COLUMN 1	*COLUMN 2*	ANSWERS	SCORE
(A) beneficiary	1. The person who turns over property to be held and managed in a trust.	________	1.______
(B) estate planning	2. A trust set up to take effect during a person's lifetime.	________	2.______
(C) living trust	3. Having assets that may be readily converted into cash.	________	3.______
(D) marital deduction	4. The person who holds and manages the property in a trust.	________	4.______
(E) settlor	5. A person who receives benefits under a trust agreement.	________	5.______
(F) trust	6. A trust set up after death through a will.	________	6.______
(G) trustee	7. A federal estate tax deduction available when property is transferred to a spouse under certain conditions.	________	7.______
(H) net estate	8. The process of planning for the management and disposition of one's assets to dispose of them properly and to minimize income and estate taxes.	________	8.______
(I) testamentary trust	9. A device used to transfer property for the purpose of holding and managing it for the benefit of another.	________	9.______
(J) liquidity	10. Assets left by an individual at death, less certain deductions permitted by law.	________	10.______

PART 3: Answer the following questions in the space provided. *SCORE*

1. List the person(s) who should be consulted in developing an estate plan.

____

____

______________________________ 1. ______

2. List and describe briefly the steps involved in developing an estate plan.

____

____

____

____

______________________________ 2. ______

3. Describe the four different types of transfers to a spouse that might qualify for the marital deduction.

____

____

____

______________________________ 3. ______

4. List and describe three different devices that might be used to minimize estate taxes.

____

____

____

____

____

______________________________ 4. ______

Activity—Keeping Financial and Legal Records

Whether you are planning your estate or just keeping good financial records, you need to know what legal documents you have and where they are. On the following two pages is a form for taking an inventory of financial information and legal records. Although the information asked for may not all be applicable to you right now, fill out as much of the form as you can. You may want to keep this inventory as a quick reference to your own financial and legal records.

KEY PERSONAL PAPERS

Name	Location
Certificates birth	
adoption	
baptismal	
marriage	
Will: original copy	
Income Tax Returns	
Gift Tax Returns	
Household Inventory	
Social Security Number and Cards	
Employment Records	
Educational Records (diplomas, transcripts)	
Medical and Health Records (medication, vaccinations)	
Passport	
Citizenship Papers	
Organizations	

BANK DATA

	Name of Bank, Credit Union, etc.	Address	Account Number	Location of Bankbook (key)
Savings Accounts				
Checking Accounts				
Safe Deposit				

STOCKS, BONDS, MUTUAL FUNDS, AND OTHER INVESTMENTS

Broker ______________ Address ______________ Telephone ______________

	Issuer	Owner (Indicate whether registered or bearer)	Date of Purchase	Number of Shares	Purchase Price	Location
Stocks						
Bonds						
Other						

U.S. SAVINGS BONDS

Serial	Names Registered	Purchase Date	Purchase Price	Maturity Date	Maturity Value	Location

OTHER PERSONAL PROPERTY (car, jewelry, art, etc.)

Type of Property	Location	Insured Yes	No	Date of Purchase	Purchase Price

REAL ESTATE AND OTHER ASSETS

Description and Location	Date of Purchase	Purchase Price	Title in Name of	Mortgage Amount/Holder	Location of Records

INSURANCE

Broker/Agent ______________________ Address ____ Telephone ________

	Company and Address	Policy Number	Location of Policy	Type of Insurance	Beneficiary	Value on Natural Death	Value on Accidental Death
Life Insurance							
Health Insurance							
Home/Car Insurance							
Other							

DEBTS (Bank, mortgage, broker, and insurance loans, installment contracts)

Creditor's Name and Address	Amount	Collateral, if any	Location of Records and Documents

UNIT 10 WILLS AND ESTATE PLANNING

Review

NAME____________________ DATE________

SCORE________

Review

PART 1: Indicate whether each statement below is true or false by circling either "true" or "false" in the Answers column.

	ANSWERS	SCORE
1. A person may dispose of her or his estate without restriction.	true false	1.____
2. If a person who makes a will destroys it, this act usually makes a prior will become effective.	true false	2.____
3. If a will is properly witnessed, a codicil to that will need not be witnessed.	true false	3.____
4. If a surviving spouse does not receive a certain amount under a will, that spouse may elect to disregard the will and take the share that would have been received had the deceased died without a will.	true false	4.____
5. A bequest in a will to one's children will not be shared by children born after the will is executed.	true false	5.____
6. Before a will becomes effective, its validity must be proven in a court of law.	true false	6.____
7. Alteration of a will before it is signed and witnessed invalidates it.	true false	7.____
8. If a person dies leaving an insurance policy whose proceeds are payable to a named beneficiary, that person will receive those proceeds regardless of the terms of the deceased person's will.	true false	8.____
9. A person who is physically incapable of signing a will may "sign" it using an "X" in place of a signature.	true false	9.____
10. The administrator of an estate of a person who dies intestate has the same functions as an executor of an estate of a person who dies leaving a will.	true false	10.____
11. A provision in a will that requires a beneficiary to remain single is not valid.	true false	11.____
12. If a person bequeaths a specific automobile and that car is sold before the person dies, the bequest is ineffective.	true false	12.____
13. The age requirement for making a valid will is determined as of the date of making the will, not as of the date of death.	true false	13.____
14. If a will is declared invalid, the executor determines how that person's estate will be distributed.	true false	14.____
15. Making gifts helps to save on income taxes but has no effect on minimizing estate taxes.	true false	15.____

PART 2: For each statement, write the letter of the best answer in the Answers column.

	ANSWERS	SCORE
1. Disposition of an intestate's property is determined by (A) state law, (B) provisions of the will, (C) federal law, (D) custom.	____	1.____
2. Selection of an executor to handle an estate is made by (A) the judge of the surrogate court, (B) the person who executed the will, (C) the beneficiaries, (D) the spouse of the deceased.	____	2.____
3. To be valid, a handwritten will (A) need not be witnessed, (B) must be witnessed by one person, (C) must be witnessed by two people, (D) must be witnessed by three people.	____	3.____
4. In an oral will, a person may dispose of (A) real property only, (B) real and personal property, (C) personal property only, (D) none of these answers.	____	4.____
5. To be valid, a will must be signed by the maker (A) at the beginning, (B) on each page, (C) immediately before the witnesses' signatures, (D) at the very end of the will.	____	5.____

PART 3: For each of the following case problems, give a decision by writing "yes" or "no" in the space provided. Then, in sentence form, give a reason for your decision.

SCORE

1. Perkins typed a will and then added his handwritten signature at the end. The will was not witnessed. In this will, Perkins left all of his property to his sister. Perkins's other sister claimed that the will was void. Is she correct?

Decision: ______________________________

Reason: ______________________________

______________________________ 1. ______

2. Nichols executed a will valid in all respects. In the will, she left $5,000 to her nephew. Six months later, Nichols crossed out this figure and wrote in $50,000. When Nichols died, the nephew made a claim against the estate for $50,000. Is the claim valid?

Decision: ______________________________

Reason: ______________________________

______________________________ 2. ______

3. Burdine left a will in which she bequeathed her house to her sister, provided she agreed to live in the house and not sell it. On Burdine's death, the sister claimed that this provision was invalid. Is she correct?

Decision: ______________________________

Reason: ______________________________

______________________________ 3. ______

4. Gregg executed a will leaving all of his property to his wife and two children. When he made the will, he had two children. A year later another child was born, but Gregg never changed his will. When Gregg died, the first two children claimed that the third child was not entitled to share in Gregg's estate. Are they correct?

Decision: ______________________________

Reason: ______________________________

______________________________ 4. ______

PART 4: In the Answers column at the right, write the letter of the word or words in Column 1 that best match each statement in Column 2.

COLUMN 1	*COLUMN 2*	*ANSWERS*	*SCORE*
(A) probate	1. The personal representative of a deceased named in the deceased's will.	______	1. ______
(B) trust	2. An addition or amendment to a will.	______	2. ______
(C) intestate	3. The process of validating a will in surrogate or probate court.	______	3. ______
(D) executor	4. A person who dies without a will.	______	4. ______
(E) codicil	5. A plan by which one turns over property to someone to hold and manage for another.	______	5. ______

UNIT 11 BUSINESS ORGANIZATION AND REGULATION

Chapter 40 Sole Proprietorships and Partnerships

NAME____________________________________ DATE____________

SCORE____________

Study Guide and Review

PART 1: Answer each of the following questions by circling either "yes" or "no" in the Answers column.

	ANSWERS		SCORE
1. Is the sole proprietorship the most flexible form of business organization?	yes	no	1.______
2. In most states, are any formalities required to establish a sole proprietorship?	yes	no	2.______
3. Must a sole proprietor using a trade name register that name in a public office?	yes	no	3.______
4. May lawyers or doctors practice their professions in partnerships?	yes	no	4.______
5. To establish a partnership, must there always be a partnership agreement?	yes	no	5.______
6. If a partnership is formed by an agreement, must the agreement be in writing?	yes	no	6.______
7. In the absence of any agreement, can a partnership be implied from the actions of the partners?	yes	no	7.______
8. If a partnership wishes to admit new partners, must all of the existing partners agree to the change?	yes	no	8.______
9. Is it possible for all partners in a partnership to share equally in the profits even if they do not equally share management responsibilities?	yes	no	9.______
10. If there are three partners in a business, may one of them sell one third of the assets to someone else?	yes	no	10.______

PART 2: Answer the following questions in the space provided below. *SCORE*

1. Explain the difference between a trading and a nontrading partnership.

____

____ 1.______

2. List and explain briefly five different types of partners.

____

____

____

____ 2.______

3. Explain the basic difference between a general partnership and a limited partnership.

____

____

____ 3.______

PART 3: For each statement, write the letter of the best answer in the Answers column. ANSWERS SCORE

1. The most common form of business organization is the (A) corporation, (B) limited partnership, (C) sole proprietorship, (D) partnership. ________ 1.______
2. An inactive partner known by the public to be a partner is called a (A) limited partner, (B) silent partner, (C) secret partner, (D) dormant partner. ________ 2.______
3. The liability of partners as a group and individually is called (A) collective liability, (B) general liability, (C) group liability, (D) joint and several liability. ________ 3.______
4. Unless otherwise agreed to, the partners' shares of the profits are (A) equal, (B) based on the amount each partner invested, (C) based on the partners' ages, (D) based on the partners' salaries. ________ 4.______
5. The termination of a partnership is called (A) disassociation, (B) cessation, (C) dis-partnership, (D) dissolution. ________ 5.______
6. When two or more persons conduct a business as a formal partnership without making a partnership agreement, they have formed (A) an express partnership, (B) a partnership by implication, (C) an illegal partnership, (D) a corporation. ________ 6.______
7. One disadvantage of a sole proprietorship is (A) lack of flexibility, (B) difficulty in setting up, (C) expense of setting up, (D) limited existence. ________ 7.______
8. A medical partnership is classified as a (A) trading partnership, (B) limited partnership, (C) joint venture, (D) nontrading partnership. ________ 8.______
9. A partnership formed to last six months (A) may be oral, (B) must be in writing, (C) is invalid, (D) is unconstitutional. ________ 9.______
10. Termination of a partnership may result from (A) death of a partner, (B) bankruptcy of a partner, (C) retirement of a partner, (D) all of these answers. ________ 10.______

PART 4: In each of the following case problems, give a decision by writing "yes" or "no" in the space provided. In sentence form give a reason for your decision. SCORE

1. Hill and Doan became partners in an automobile business. Their partnership agreement contained no provision for dividing profits and losses. At the end of the year, Hill claimed that he was entitled to more of the profits than Doan because he spent more time managing the business than Doan did. Is Hill correct?

   Decision: ____

   Reason: ____

   ____ 1.______

2. Jansen and Johnson operated a grocery store as partners. Jansen told Johnson not to buy a certain product because it was not selling well. Johnson disregarded Jansen's request and bought a large quantity. Jansen refused to pay for the product, claiming that her orders had been disregarded. Is the partnership obligated to pay for the product?

   Decision: ____

   Reason: ____

   ____ 2.______

3. Fain and Warner were partners in an automobile service station business. Because of personal business problems, Fain had to file a petition in bankruptcy. Warner claims that the partnership may continue in business. Is Warner correct?

   Decision: ____

   Reason: ____

   ____ 3.______

NAME ______________________ DATE ______________

Activity—Analyzing a Partnership Agreement

Study the partnership agreement below, then answer the questions on page 148.

PARTNERSHIP AGREEMENT

This agreement, made June 20, 19--, between Penelope Wolfburg of 783A South Street, Hazelton, Idaho, and Ingrid Swenson of RR 5, Box 96, Hazelton, Idaho.

1. The above named persons have this day formed a partnership that shall operate under the name of W-S Jewelers, located at 85 Broac Street, Hazelton, Idaho 83335, and shall engage in jewelry sales and repairs.

2. The duration of this agreement will be for a term of fifteen (15) years, beginning on June 20, 19--, or for a shorter term if agreed upon in writing by both partners.

3. The initial investment by each partner will be as follows: Penelope Wolfburg, assets and liabilities of Wolfburg's Jewelry Store, valued at a capital investment of $40,000; Ingrid Swenson, cash of $20,000. These investments are partnership property.

4. Each partner will give her time, skill, and attention to the operation of this partnership and will engage in no other business enterprise unless permission is granted in writing by the other partner.

5. The salary for each partner will be as follows: Penelope Wolfburg, $40,000 per year; Ingrid Swenson, $30,000 per year. Neither partner may withdraw cash or other assets from the business without express permission in writing from the other partner. All profits and losses of the business will be shared as follows: Penelope Wolfburg, 60 percent; Ingrid Swenson, 40 percent.

6. Upon the dissolution of the partnership due to termination of this agreement, or to written permission by each of the partners, or to the death or incapacitation of one or both partners, a new contract may be entered into by the partners or the sole continuing partner has the option to purchase the other partner's interest in the business at a price that shall not exceed the balance in the terminating partner's capital account. The payment shall be made in cash in equal quarterly installments from the date of termination.

7. At the conclusion of this contract, unless it is agreed by both partners to continue the operation of the business under a new contract, the assets of the partnership, after the liabilities are paid, will be divided in proportion to the balance in each partner's capital account on that date.

Penelope Wolfburg	*Ingrid Swenson*
Penelope Wolfburg	Ingrid Swenson
June 20, 19--	*June 20, 19--*
Date	Date

SCORE

1. Under the statue of frauds, could this agreement have been oral?

1. ______

2. What restriction does this agreement place on the partners' ability to pursue other business enterprises?

2. ______

3. How will the partners share the profits and losses of the business?

3. ______

4. Swenson wants to borrow $2,000 from the assets of the business. Does the partnership agreement allow her to do so?

4. ______

5. Wolfburg learned that a large jewelry collection was to be auctioned off at an estate sale. She bought several items at the auction and then resold them at a considerable profit. Is Wolfburg correct in claiming that she is not required to share the earnings from this transaction with Swenson?

5. ______

6. What provisions does the agreement list for terminating the partnership?

6. ______

UNIT 11 BUSINESS ORGANIZATION AND REGULATION

Chapter 41 Corporations

NAME______________________________ DATE__________

SCORE__________

Study Guide and Review

PART 1: For each of the following case problems, give a decision by writing "yes" or "no" in the space provided. Then, in sentence form, give a reason for your decision. *SCORE*

1. The directors of the Brennan Corporation were negligent in handling the corporation's business, and the company lost money. The stockholders then voted to dissolve the corporation. Do the common stockholders have first claim against the assets?

   Decision: ______________________________

   Reason: ______________________________

   ____

   ____

   ______________________________ 1.______

2. The Rogers Corporation was organized to manufacture electronic equipment. The board of directors voted (a) to borrow $1,000,000 to expand the company and (b) to go into the plumbing business. Neither action was authorized by the charter and bylaws. Can the stockholders invalidate both these actions?

   Decision: ______________________________

   Reason: ______________________________

   ____

   ____

   ______________________________ 2.______

PART 2: In the Answers column at the right, write the letter of the word or words in Column 1 that best match each statement in Column 2.

COLUMN 1	*COLUMN 2*	*ANSWERS*	*SCORE*
(A) board of directors	1. The written permission given by stockholders to someone else to vote for them.	______	1.______
(B) preferred stock	2. A type of stock entitled to receive dividends provided profits are earned.	______	2.______
(C) dividend	3. The joining of two corporations, with one surviving.	______	3.______
(D) proxy	4. Stock having a prior right to receive a dividend.	______	4.______
(E) ultra vires	5. Acts of a corporation that exceed its powers.	______	5.______
(F) common stock	6. The application for permission to incorporate.	______	6.______
(G) stock certificate	7. A person having an interest in a corporation.	______	7.______
(H) stockholder	8. The group that sets corporate policy.	______	8.______
(I) merger	9. A document showing part ownership of a corporation.	______	9.______
(J) articles of incorporation	10. A part of corporate profits paid to stockholders.	______	10.______

PART 3: For each statement, write the letter of the best answer in the Answers column. *ANSWERS* *SCORE*

1. To organize a corporation, permission is first required from (A) the court, (B) the state government, (C) a judge, (D) the federal government. ________ 1.______
2. A corporation that is organized in one state and does business there is known in that state as (A) a local corporation, (B) a foreign corporation, (C) a regional corporation, (D) a domestic corporation. ________ 2.______
3. The first formal step in incorporating a corporation is the drafting and filing of the (A) articles of incorporation, (B) company bylaws, (C) stock certificates, (D) minutes of incorporation. ________ 3.______
4. The number, type, and nature of stock issued by a corporation are known collectively as its (A) liquidity factor, (B) stock composition, (C) capitalization, (D) no par factor ________ 4.______
5. Corporate stock that has a prior claim to dividends over all other classes of stock is called (A) cumulative stock, (B) participating stock, (C) no-par stock, (D) preferred stock. ________ 5.______
6. General policy for a corporation is determined by the (A) stockholders, (B) legislature, (C) directors, (D) New York Stock Exchange. ________ 6.______
7. Officers of a corporation are hired by the (A) directors, (B) stockholders, (C) state, (D) other officers. ________ 7.______
8. Most corporations are incorporated for (A) a term of 10 years, (B) a term of 100 years, (C) an indefinite term, (D) a term of 75 years. ________ 8.______
9. When two corporations join together and a new one is formed, the result is known as (A) a merger, (B) a joint venture, (C) an amalgamation, (D) a consolidation. ________ 9.______
10. Corporate existence ends if (A) the corporate term ends, (B) the stockholders agree it should, (C) the charter is revoked, (D) any of these answers. ________ 10.______
11. When one corporation buys another corporation, the purchase is known as (A) a consolidation, (B) a merger, (C) an amalgamation, (D) a proxy. ________ 11.______
12. A corporation organized to operate a state hospital would be an example of a (A) public corporation, (B) nonprofit corporation, (C) common stock corporation, (D) municipal corporation. ________ 12.______
13. If a corporation organized to build homes began selling used cars instead, the action would be considered (A) sua sponte, (B) de bonis non, (C) ultra vires, (D) inter vivos. ________ 13.______
14. An Idaho corporation doing business in Ohio is considered, in Ohio, (A) a domestic corporation, (B) a foreign corporation, (C) an invalid corporation, (D) a common stock corporation. ________ 14.______
15. Directors of a corporation are elected by the (A) stockholders, (B) state, (C) officers, (D) federal government. ________ 15.______
16. A stockholder's written authorization allowing another person to cast her or his vote is called (A) ultra vires, (B) a stock certificate, (C) pre-emptive right, (D) a proxy. ________ 16.______
17. Nonprofit corporations can be organized (A) to provide charitable services, (B) to earn money, (C) to operate without a charter, (D) to issue stock. ________ 17.______
18. The board of directors of a corporation is usually elected for a period of (A) 1 year, (B) 2 years, (C) 5 years, (D) 10 years. ________ 18.______
19. Two types of private corporations are (A) stock/nonstock, (B) profit/nonprofit, (C) limited/general, (D) common/preferred. ________ 19.______
20. All stockholders in a corporation have the right to (A) receive dividends, (B) vote on corporate matters, (C) sell their stock, (D) establish corporate policy. ________ 20.______

NAME____ DATE______________

Activity—Word Search

The 14 words listed below are important terms relating to the operation of corporations. These words can be found in the word search puzzle below. The words read forward, backward, up, down, and diagonally, but always in a straight line and never skipping letters. Circle each word you find.

SCORE

P	C	E	R	T	I	F	I	C	A	T	E	S	A
R	A	C	O	R	P	O	R	A	T	I	O	N	C
S	P	R	O	X	Y	V	O	A	W	A	O	O	Y
A	I	F	Q	G	T	F	E	N	L	M	N	N	U
S	T	O	C	K	H	L	D	R	M	S	B	P	L
D	A	H	C	L	A	K	R	O	O	B	S	R	T
E	L	K	A	R	T	I	C	L	E	S	F	O	R
R	I	D	Z	M	L	B	I	K	J	Y	X	F	A
R	Z	D	I	V	I	D	E	N	D	S	H	I	V
E	A	C	B	F	A	A	M	S	C	K	O	T	I
F	T	H	E	T	B	S	L	M	E	R	G	E	R
E	I	N	I	I	T	A	X	O	P	G	O	C	E
R	O	O	W	B	R	N	A	L	H	C	P	A	S
P	N	O	P	A	R	S	T	O	C	K	K	C	B

articles
capitalization
certificate
consolidation
common
corporation
dividend
merger
nonprofit
no par stock
preferred
proxy
stock
ultra vires

______

PART 4: Read the following paragraph, then answer the questions on page 152.

Salerno and Peterson organized a corporation in Indiana to manufacture and market solar heating panels. They chose the name Icarus, Inc., even though there was already a company in Indiana named Icarus, Ltd., that manufactured sunglasses. They planned to issue 200,000 shares of stock in the corporation. Also, in drawing up the bylaws, Salerno wanted to include a provision that in the event of his death, the corporation would be dissolved.

1. Will Salerno and Peterson be allowed to use the name Icarus, Inc.?

SCORE

1. ______

2. What are the advantages of organizing this company as a corporation rather than as a partnership?

2. ______

3. Can Salerno insist that in the event of his death the corporation must be dissolved?

3. ______

4. Like most corporations, this company will be subject to "double taxation." Explain the double taxation of corporations.

4. ______

5. Cortillo bought 1500 shares of stock in the corporation. After one year, the company declared an annual dividend of $1.25 per share. How much will Cortillo receive in dividends as a result?

5. ______

6. Describe the ways in which this corporation can be dissolved.

6. ______

UNIT 11 BUSINESS ORGANIZATION AND REGULATION

Chapter 42 Government Regulation of Business

NAME________________________________

DATE____________

SCORE____________

Study Guide and Review

PART 1 For each statement write the letter of the best answer in the Answers column.

	ANSWERS	SCORE
1. Government regulation of business is designed to protect (A) consumers, (B) employees, (C) stockholders, (D) all of these answers.	________	1. ______
2. The basic power to regulate business that federal, state, and local governments possess is known as the (A) commerce power, (B) police power, (C) regulatory power, (D) public power.	________	2. ______
3. Business activity that is conducted solely within the boundaries of a state is known as (A) domestic commerce, (B) interstate commerce, (C) intrastate commerce, (D) foreign commerce.	________	3. ______
4. The power to regulate interstate commerce comes from (A) the individual states, (B) the United States Constitution, (C) local government, (D) the United Nations Charter.	________	4. ______
5. Antitrust regulation at the federal level is based on the (A) Sherman Act, (B) Jackson Act, (C) Nixon Act, (D) Reagan Act.	________	5. ______
6. The Federal Trade Commission Act of 1914 prohibits (A) monopolies, (B) mergers, (C) price discrimination (D) unfair competition.	________	6. ______
7. The antitrust laws apply to all the following organizations except (A) labor unions, (B) railroads, (C) steel companies, (D) lumber companies.	________	7. ______
8. Most governmental regulations of business are enforced by (A) the police, (B) local government, (C) administrative agencies, (D) the United States Congress.	________	8. ______
9. The sale and trading of securities is regulated by (A) the Federal Reserve Board, (B) the New York Stock Exchange, (C) the Securities and Exchange Commission, (D) the Bank of the United States.	________	9. ______
10. Laws prohibiting the sale of certain products on certain days of the week are known as (A) sunshine laws, (B) closing laws, (C) common laws, (D) Sunday laws.	________	10. ______

PART 2: Answer the following questions in the space provided. SCORE

1. List five important areas in which government regulates business to protect the public.

____

____ 1. ______

2. Administrative agencies have legislative, executive, and judicial powers. Give a brief explanation of each type of power.

____

____

____ 2. ______

PART 3: Read the case problems below and then state what agency or agencies you might consult for help in each situation.

SCORE

1. You operate a retail store selling musical instruments. A large chain store that also sells musical instruments opens for business a few blocks from your store. The owners of that store spread a rumor that your pianos are made of inferior materials and will not last more than six months.

   Agency: ______________________________ 1. ______

2. You work for a machine tool company and operate a lathe. It is common practice for employers to provide employees with safety glasses to prevent injury caused by pieces of metal being thrown from the machines. Your employer, however, refuses to provide you with this type of safety equipment.

   Agency: ______________________________ 2. ______

3. You buy 50,000 shares of stock in a uranium mining company and then discover that the company had not disclosed the fact that uranium had never been found in the area in which the company planned to do business. You want to return the stock and get your money back, but the company refuses.

   Agency: ______________________________ 3. ______

4. You are chairperson of a federal government agency responsible for protecting those who borrow money from banks. You learn that a certain bank has been charging its borrowers an interest rate that is double the maximum permitted by federal law.

   Agency: ______________________________ 4. ______

5. You live in a city in which there are four television stations. One company purchases all four stations and broadcasts the same news on all the stations. You feel that the public interest is not being served by this monopoly practice.

   Agency: ______________________________ 5. ______

6. You live in a residential area that is zoned for one-family houses only. A local manufacturer buys the three homes next to yours and announces that it plans to demolish the homes and erect a factory.

   Agency: ______________________________ 6. ______

7. You go to a doctor for treatment of a skin condition. Two weeks later you discover that your doctor never graduated from medical school and was never licensed to practice medicine in your state.

   Agency: ______________________________ 7. ______

8. You apply for telephone service and are advised that a $200 deposit is required before you can obtain service. You believe that the deposit amount is excessive and unfair, but the phone company refuses to provide you with service unless you pay the deposit.

   Agency: ______________________________ 8. ______

UNIT 11 BUSINESS ORGANIZATION AND REGULATION

Review

NAME________________________ DATE__________

SCORE__________

Review

PART 1: Indicate whether each statement below is true or false by circling either "true" or "false" in the Answers column.

	ANSWERS		SCORE
1. A sole proprietor often may have to obtain a license to engage in certain businesses.	true	false	1.______
2. In some states, a partnership may sue or be sued in its own name.	true	false	2.______
3. A partnership is considered a legal entity for tax purposes.	true	false	3.______
4. A partnership is bound by any contracts entered into by an individual partner, regardless of the type of contract.	true	false	4.______
5. Most corporations prohibit voting by proxy at annual stockholders' meetings.	true	false	5.______
6. In most states voting by stockholders is on a one-vote-per-share basis.	true	false	6.______
7. A stockholder has the right, subject to reasonable rules and regulations, to inspect corporate records for the purpose of trying to replace the present members of the board of directors with new directors.	true	false	7.______
8. In most states a director is not liable for contracts or for negligence in connection with acts performed on the corporation's behalf.	true	false	8.______
9. Both the state and federal governments have the power to regulate business and to protect the rights of consumers and stockholders.	true	false	9.______
10. The government may prohibit all monopolies, even those that arise out of lawful and reasonable acts.	true	false	10.______

PART 2: For each statement, write the letter of the best answer in the Answers column.

	ANSWERS	SCORE
1. The most easily started form of business organization is the (A) general partnership, (B) corporation, (C) limited partnership, (D) sole proprietorship.	________	1.______
2. In most states, a sole proprietor must register a business or trade name in (A) the local Chamber of Commerce, (B) a local bank, (C) a public office, (D) Washington, D.C.	________	2.______
3. A partner who is neither active in a partnership nor known to the public as a partner is called (A) silent, (B) dormant, (C) general, (D) secret.	________	3.______
4. The major difference between a general partnership and a limited partnership is (A) degree of liability, (B) degree of management, (C) amount of investment, (D) percentage of ownership.	________	4.______
5. A business corporation may (A) borrow money in its own name, (B) sue and be sued in its own name, (C) own property in its own name, (D) all of these answers.	________	5.______
6. Public utilities are chartered by (A) city or town governments only, (B) state governments only, (C) the federal government only, (D) both state and federal government.	________	6.______
7. Officers of a corporation are chosen by the (A) stockholders, (B) directors, (C) previous officers, (D) trustees.	________	7.______
8. The life of a corporation is *not* affected by (A) mergers, (B) death of a stockholder, (C) court decree, (D) consolidation.	________	8.______
9. Laws enacted to prevent monopolies are known as (A) ultra vires laws, (B) merger laws, (C) antitrust laws, (D) OSHA laws.	________	9.______
10. A local zoning board is an example of (A) a corporation, (B) a monopoly, (C) an administrative agency, (D) a public utility.	________	10.______

PART 3: In the Answers column at the right, write the letter of the word or words in Column 1 that best match each statement in Column 2.

COLUMN 1	COLUMN 2	ANSWERS	SCORE
(A) joint and several liability	1. Stock with no stated value.	______	1. ______
(B) joint venture	2. Liability of partners as a group and individually.	______	2. ______
(C) no-par stock	3. Power of a state to protect the welfare of its citizens.	______	3. ______
(D) treble damages	4. An association of two or more companies engaged in a common venture.	______	4. ______
(E) police power	5. Damages payable for violation of the antitrust laws.	______	5. ______

PART 4: In each of the following case problems, give a decision by writing "yes" or "no" in the space provided. Then, in sentence form, give a reason for your decision.

SCORE

1. Curry, Davis, and Ivy were partners operating a motel. Davis died and Ivy and Curry decided to continue to operate the business. Was it legally necessary for them to make a new partnership agreement?

Decision: ______________________________

Reason: ______________________________

______________________________ 1. ______

2. Pillson, a partner in a retail drug business, was responsible for purchasing drugs from wholesalers. One wholesaler gave Pillson a 5% commission in appreciation for the order placed for the partnership. Was Pillson entitled to keep the commission for personal use?

Decision: ______________________________

Reason: ______________________________

______________________________ 2. ______

3. Granby was treasurer of the Eagle Electric Corp. The company owed $10,000 for electric cable purchased by the corporation for use in its business. An action was brought against Granby for payment of the $10,000. Is Granby liable?

Decision: ______________________________

Reason: ______________________________

______________________________ 3. ______

4. Hill and Fox each owned 50% of the shares of stock of the Ames Corp. Hill died and left the stock to her family. Is it necessary for Fox to set up a new corporation to be able to continue in business?

Decision: ______________________________

Reason: ______________________________

______________________________ 4. ______

